Every Play Revealed
Volume II:
New England vs Seattle

ALEX KIRBY

ISBN: 978-1516846740
ISBN-13: 1516846745

CONTENTS

Player Numbers

New England

11—Julian Edelman
12—Tom Brady
19—Brandon LaFell
21—Malcolm Butler
23—Patrick Chung
24—Darrelle Revis
34—Shane Vereen
38—Brandon Bolden
46—James Develin
47—Michael Hoomanawanui
80—Danny Amendola
81—Tim Wright
87—Rob Gronkowski

Seattle

3—Russell Wilson
13—Chris Matthews
15—Jermaine Kearse
19—Bryan Walters
22—Robert Turbin
25—Richard Sherman
31—Kam Chancellor
82—Luke Wilson
83—Ricardo Lockette
84—Cooper Helfet
88—Tony Moeaki
89—Doug Baldwin

<u>Key to Defensive Symbols</u>

E	Defensive End
T	Defensive Tackle
N	Nose Tackle
B	Strong Outside Linebacker/Standup Defensive End
S	Sam Linebacker
M	Mike Linebacker
W	Will Linebacker
C	Corner
FS	Free Safety
SS	Strong Safety
WS	Weak Safety
NS	Nickel Safety

PREGAME POINTS OF EMPHASIS:
NEW ENGLAND OFFENSE

Test out the defense early with multiple formations, motions, and personnel groupings-

New England is one of the few teams in the NFL who have the ability to be truly multiple on offense. With the two-headed monster of LaGarrette Blount and Shane Vereen in the backfield each serving a specific purpose within the offense, along with Rob Gronkowski and Julian Edelman, the Patriots can line up in so many different looks and have receivers who are multi-talented as blockers and pass-catchers. Fortunately for New England they've been moving between different formations all season long, so there's nothing they'll be asked to do in this game that they won't have experience with.

Use compressed formations to create space out on the edge, and force the perimeter defenders to be wrong no matter what-

Obviously New England is going to keep a close eye on the right side of the field, where Richard Sherman has made a habit of lining up all season long, but they're going to have to have a plan in place to attack the opposite side of the field as well.

By moving the single receiver in tighter, how far can they get the defenders to move in with them? At the same time, how much room can they create on the perimeter for the offensive skill players? Can Josh McDaniels and this Patriots offense construct a scenario whereby compressing the formation they end up outflanking the defense on the edge? Will they be able to affect the linebackers inside the box, moving them side to side and getting them to vacate their assigned gaps to open up space for the run game?

This is what New England will have to find out early on in the game.

Find a way to throw the shallow crossing route and create yards after the catch -

Any coach who watched even a couple of games worth of film on this Patriot offense could tell you that one of their biggest "bread-and-butter" plays is the shallow crossing route. Thus, Seattle no doubt has a plan for how to stop it, and it's Josh McDaniels' job to figure out what that plan is and devise a way to defeat it.

Central to New England's ability to throw the shallow cross is finding ways to open up the middle of the field, and one of the most important plays in that endeavor is running back Shane Vereen. If Vereen can present himself as a dangerous threat out of the backfield to catch the football, then the defense will have to assign underneath defenders to take him away in the pass game instead of standing guard underneath in the middle of the tackle box.

PREGAME POINTS OF EMPHASIS: NEW ENGLAND DEFENSE

Slow down Lynch -

Notice the wording of that statement, it doesn't say "stop" Lynch, it says to slow him down. Marshawn Lynch is one of the best backs in the league, and often it takes more than a single tackler to bring him down.

But how exactly can the Patriots accomplish this. Simply put, they've got to get more bodies to the football than Seattle can block, as well as get more tacklers on Lynch than he can handle. One specific way is through Bill Belichick's strategic use of 2-gap defensive tackles and aggressive play from the inside linebackers. Belichick and his defensive coordinator Matt Patricia devised specific defensive fronts that, at least on paper, will allow the defense to get an unblocked defender to the ball on every play.

Thanks to film study and excellent preparation, New England is able to give their inside linebackers a very specific set of instructions based on how the Seattle backfield is aligned. This is the genius of Bill Belichick's coaching style, not only is he able to zero in on what you do best and take it away, he's also able to present the information to his players in a way that will not overwhelm them and allows them to play fast and aggressive.

The next page contains some examples of how New England will react to the shotgun run game out of different alignments, and how each linebacker has his own instructions.

As you can see, the defense is set up to provide pursuit and a bonus guy to the run since all gaps are taken care of, and they've even got the weak side DE assigned to peel off with the back on a flare route if that happens.

Clearly Belichick has his defense coached up in this area.

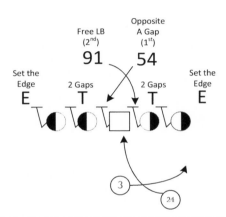

BASIC RUN FITS

In this balanced front, the interior of the line of scrimmage is supposed to be controlled by the two defensive tackles. The run fits by the defensive ends are determined by the inside linebackers playing behind them. In the diagram to the left, the assume the offensive strength is set to the right. Hightower will almost always align to the tight end strength of the formation, and when the back is to his side, his job is to attack the opposite A-gap, and prevent the center from climbing to the second level and sealing off #91 Jamie Collins. Collins should be unblocked at this point, and free to go get the running back.

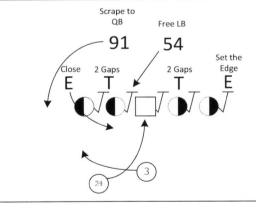

Shotgun – RB aligned strong

Much of this was covered just above, but it's important to know that the unblocked DE will play up the field, but still remain careful not to create too wide a running lane to his inside. He wants to take away any angle for Russell Wilson to get to the edge on the zone read keeper.

To the opposite side, the left DE in this diagram is also responsible for setting the edge and preventing the runner from cutting to the outside.

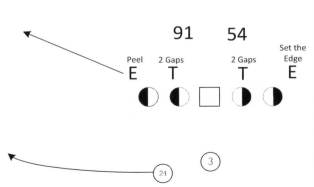

Shotgun – RB aligned weak (Run Game)

Since Collins is the speedier of the two inside linebackers, Belichick feels that he is better equipped to take on Wilson on the edge in the run game whenever he runs the zone read play. Collins is still responsible for coming up the field on the proper angle to cut off any outside runs and turn Wilson back inside if he keeps it to the left.

To the opposite side, Hightower is now the free linebacker responsible for seeking out the ball carrier since all gaps are occupied right now.

Shotgun – RB aligned weak (Pass Game)

In this case, Belichick has coached up the weakside DE to peel off on the edge if the back flares out or otherwise runs a route to the weakside.

This tactic ensures that the defense will still have numerical superiority to the weak side, and so that the secondary won't have to worry about taking the back in pass coverage. This has the added benefit of drawing a defender into the passing window when the offense is trying to run a slant to that same side behind the defender.

Take away the middle of the field and force Wilson to make the long throws deep and out on the perimeter -

When putting together a defensive game plan, especially at the professional level, a coach's job is to choose between the lesser of two (or more) evils. Questions like "who would you rather have with the ball in their hands?" and "what throws would you prefer the QB not have available?"

In this same way Bill Belichick has to decide what he's most comfortable with Russell Wilson having available to him, because realistically he's not going to be able to take away the entire field.

Russell Wilson is a good professional quarterback, having led his team to two-straight Super Bowl appearances, but Belichick believes there are some weaknesses in his game, and furthermore, the Seattle receiving corps is not particularly deep either, meaning that if the Patriots defense can take away the middle of the field with a mix of robber coverages and use of underneath defenders to take away the high-percentage throws in the middle of the field, Seattle will have a much tougher time moving the ball consistently against this defense.

Keep Russell Wilson in the pocket-

As we talked about earlier with point #1, New England's game plan for their defensive ends revolves around their ability to set a definitive edge to both side, coming up the field and preventing Russell Wilson from getting out of containment when dropping back to pass.

This is the same reason they're playing so far up the field against zone-read type plays, or any kind of play where the backside end is unblocked. Belichick wants to make the choice very obvious for Russell Wilson when running any kind of read play for the most part, so that he hands it off to Lynch up the middle and they don't have to deal with Wilson's speed on the edge.

If they can do these three things they've got a great chance to be successful.

PREGAME POINTS OF EMPHASIS: SEATTLE OFFENSE

Win 1st down -

Offensive coordinator Darrell Bevell knows that getting in 3rd and long situations against this Patriots defense is asking for trouble. Fortunately for him he's got one of the best backs in the league for running downhill at a defensive front and getting yards after contact.

If Seattle can consistently pick up four yards on 1st down, mostly by relying on the legs of Marshawn Lynch, then 2nd and 3rd down won't be as daunting for this offense. Bevell knows that Seattle does not want to be put into a position where they have to rely on Russell Wilson's arm. As talented a player and an athlete as he is, Wilson is at his best with a strong running game to set him up for success.

Use specific personnel groups to create mismatches on defense -

This goes well beyond the simple idea that the offense has to spread out the defense and create one-on-one matchups, it's much more than that.

Bill Belichick's game plan is built around identifying and responding to the personnel group that the offense has on the field at any given time (which isn't unique, since most defensive coaches follow a similar plan), however when you bring on a certain group of players, like personnel packages that include a fullback for example, there are going to be some assumptions made by the defense.

For one thing, it's assumed that when a fullback comes onto the field, the QB is likely to be under center, maybe in the I-Formation, for a power run game attack.

In this way, Seattle can bring on personnel that lends itself more to a two-back set and line up in a one-back set, and in the process exploit defensive fronts and coverages that are designed with the assumption that the offense will line up and pound the football up the middle. If you come onto the field with two tight ends and two backs, then line up in a one-back formation, you have the potential to cause problems for a defense.

Be physical in the pass game -

That's not a typo, it really will be important for Seattle to be physical with the defense when Wilson drops back to pass.

None of the receivers on Seattle's roster were drafted, and while guys like Jermain Kearse and Doug Baldwin are good enough to start in the NFL, Seattle doesn't have a receiver who can really make defensive coordinator nervous. Seahawks offensive coordinator Darrell Bevell knows that Bill Belichick will challenge Seattle's receivers to beat them, and that likely means a lot of press-man coverage.

New England has won 3 Super Bowls under Bill Belichick, in large part because they were able to bring their physicality to the offense they were playing against, slowing them down, beating them up, and otherwise making life miserable for the opponents' offense, and particularly the skill players.

Belichick's game plan against the Rams back in 2001 is now well-known, and it's worth talking about. A large part of the Patriots' strategy involved beating up Marshall Faulk no matter where he went, even on pass plays where he was running a route and didn't get the football thrown his way. Even the defensive ends and outside linebackers, when rushing the quarterback, would make it a priority to chip and beat up Faulk as he left the backfield. Seattle expects Belichick to play their receivers much the same way, to challenge them man-to-man in aggressive coverage.

The Seahawks receiving corps needs to be prepared for this and be able to adapt.

PREGAME POINTS OF EMPHASIS: SEATTLE DEFENSE

Fly to the football/ Gang tackling -

Seattle comes into the game with the best defense in the NFL, and one that's been consistently high-performing for some time now. A large part of that has to do with their talent for flying to the football and getting multiple tacklers on the ball carrier before he can get too much momentum and get extra yards after the catch.

This will be crucial when it comes to containing guys like Shane Vereen and Julian Edelman, who make their living exploiting poor tackling and loose coverage underneath. If the defense for Seattle can limit the big plays by New England, they have a great chance of keeping the cap on this offense and preventing them from wreaking havoc on Seattle.

Be aware of where Gronk is at all times -

Rob Gronkowski is the very definition of a physical mismatch, with a combination of size, speed, and strength possessed by few others in the league. He has the size to be a nuisance in the run game by simply getting in the way of a defender and creating a running lane behind him. He has the speed to be a threat downfield in the passing game, and the body control to adjust mid-stride and go up and get the football when Brady throws it up to him.

New England will move him around and make an effort to get him the football early in order to force Seattle to account for him. Defensive coordinator Dan Quinn has a big task on his hands, since he has to be able to have enough different answers for Gronkowski to keep New England off-balance.

Whether it's using a variation of bracket coverage between multiple defenders or just lining up a linebacker or defensive back across from him, Seattle needs to be able to slow him down, because you can bet Josh McDaniels will be targeting him early and often.

Seattle Kickoff

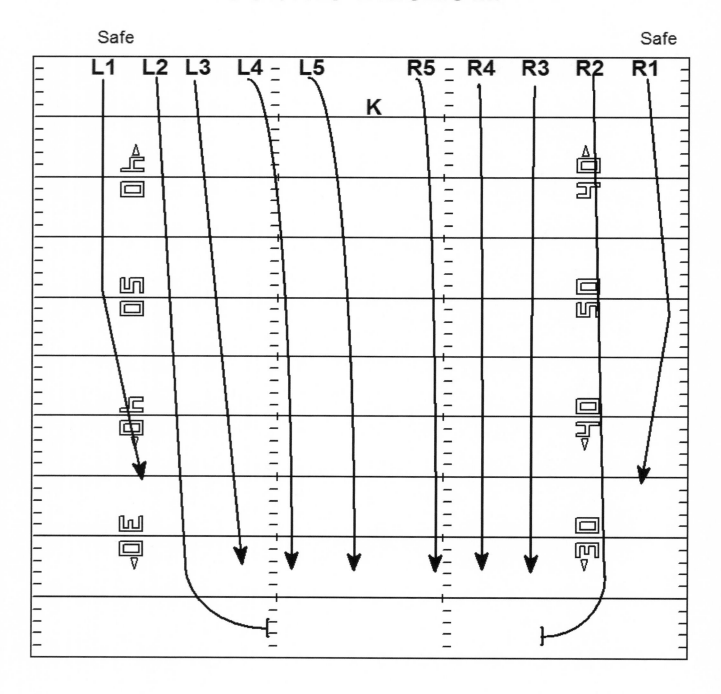

New England Kickoff Return

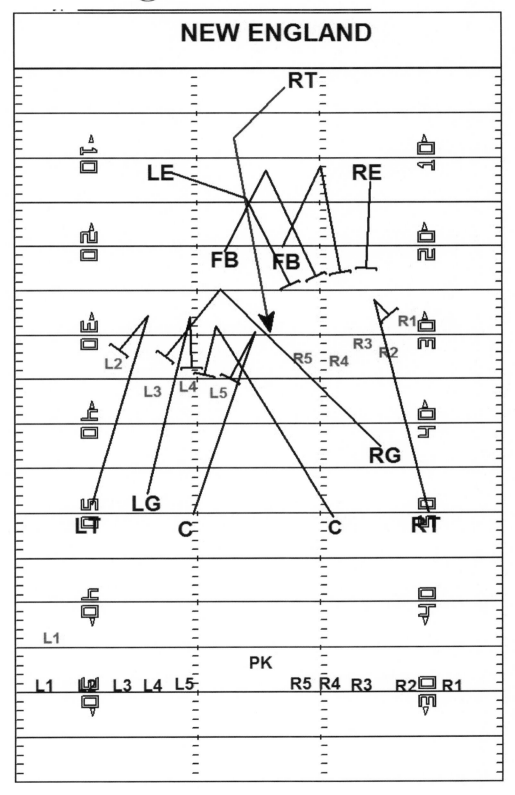

New England Drive 1 / Play 1 / 1st & 10 / -18 Yard Line / Left Hash / 14:57 1Q
NE - 0 SEA – 0

Summary

Brady completes the quick pass underneath to Gronkowski on the right side and he manages to pick up a yard before he's brought down.

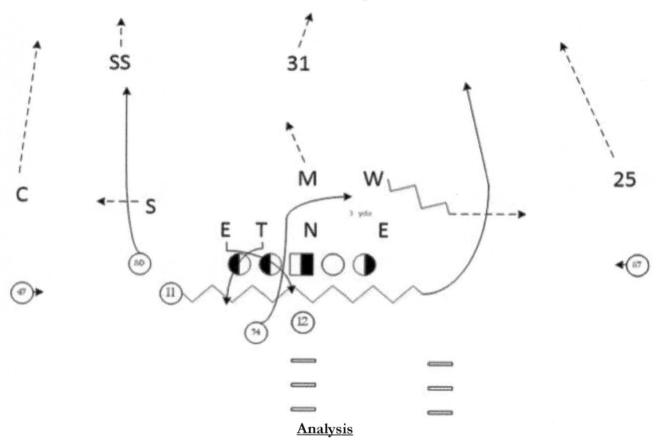

Analysis

The Patriots up in 12 personnel, with the two tight ends as the #1 receiver to each side out wide matched up on the corners. As a result, the defense to both sides ends up playing a "smash" call when they see tight ends lined up in the widest position. The corners will take a deep drop to take away any kind of out-breaking route that tries to come open behind them, and the outside backers are supposed to widen to take away the short routes by the tight ends.

The offense hopes that the wide release by the #2 receivers on both sides will create a natural rub on the outside linebackers trying to widen, and will create space on the edge for the tight end when and if he catches the ball. Of course, if the backers overplay the route and leave the inside of the vertical route open, it's an easy throw and catch for Brady.

It's also worth mentioning that Kam Chancellor doesn't move hardly at all with the motion, keeping his original position on the deep left hash, and that's something that the Patriots will take note of and have in the back of their minds as the game goes on.

New England Drive 1 / Play 2 / 2nd & 9 / -19 Yard Line / Right Hash / 14:38 1Q

NE – 0 SEA – 0

Summary

Catch by Amendola for a gain of seven yards.

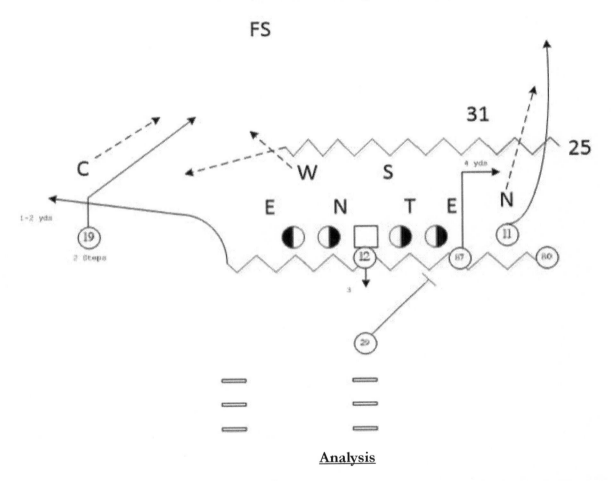

Analysis

The Patriots bring Amendola in motion from right to left and he takes Richard Sherman with him. It's a great example of New England asking as many questions as they can early on in this game and figuring out as much as possible about the structure of the defense for use later on.

The flat route by Amendola on the opposite side of the formation gets outside of Sherman and once he makes the catch he's able to shake off the tackle and pick up a few extra yards.

It should be pointed out that Sherman's depth to the right side (before the motion) allows him to run stride-for-stride with Amendola and not get tripped up in the middle while having to avoid other defenders. This is by design, since obviously the shortest distance between two points is a straight line, and if Sherman had been aligned closer to the line on the opposite side, he would've had to cover more ground in the same amount of time in order to play the motion effectively, and New England could've easily outflanked Seattle's defense by running this same motion again and again until it was corrected. Just another reason why the details matter.

New England Drive 1 / Play 3 / 3ʳᵈ & 2 / -26 Yard Line / Left Hash / 14:09 1Q

NE – 0 SEA – 0

Summary

Brady completes a pass to Vereen coming out of the backfield for the first down.

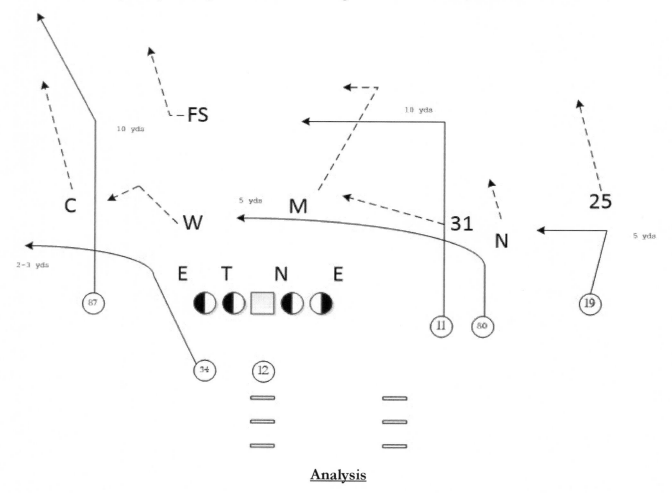

Analysis

The routes are timed up so that Vereen squares up to make his break to the outside once Gronk is even with the corner and Will linebacker and he's in a position to make an inside-breaking move, and this creates a rub on the linebacker that frees up Vereen out of the backfield. This is a variation of the smash route with Gronkowski stretching the coverage to his side and opening up space underneath.

Fortunately for Brady, his first read gets him an open receiver. In fact, this play can be read from left to right. If he doesn't like his options to the two-receiver side he can look to the receiver coming from the opposite side on the shallow crossing route and the dig route. Finally, if none of those options are open, LaFell should be breaking open underneath on the pivot route.

The Patriots also got an idea of how Kam Chancellor will align to a trips formation.

New England Drive 1 / Play 4 / 1ˢᵗ & 10 / -31 Yard Line / Left Hash / 13:32 1Q
NE – 0 SEA – 0

Summary
Gain of 2 yards by Blount on the carry to the left.

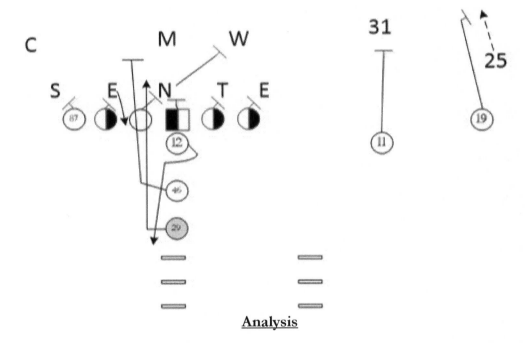

Analysis

For the first time in the game, the Patriots line up with regular personnel and put a fullback on the field.

As a response, the defense brings on an extra defensive lineman, and #51 Bruce Irvin plays more of a linebacker position on the outside shoulder of the tight end, standing up in a 2-point stance and responsible for setting the edge.

The Patriots run a simple Iso play here, with the fullback assigned to fit up on the Mike linebacker. However the defensive end lined up over the left tackle slants inside and manages to get a momentary grab on LaGarrette Blount in the backfield before he can really get moving.

The Patriots also manage to remove Chancellor from the equation by getting him to line up away from the two receiver side of the formation and then running away from him so he'll no longer be a factor.

The left tackle is forced to keep his hands on the defensive end and try to stay on him, but this just means that the nose tackle has an easier path to the ball, and Blount is tackled after a gain of two yards.

New England Drive 1 / Play 5 / 2nd & 8 / -33 Yard Line / Left Hash / 12:55 1Q
NE – 0 SEA – 0

Summary
Gain of 2 yards by Blount to the right.

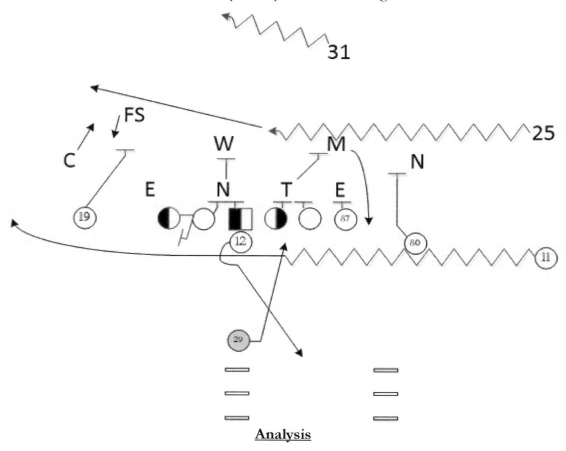

Analysis

Now the Patriots introduce another part of their run game, the inside zone scheme with a flanker sweep motion added in for good measure. One interesting thing to note about this run scheme is that the line is actually sliding to the left while the handoff to Blount is headed to the right. This is intended to induce an over pursuit by the inside linebackers and create a lane for the cutback to the left side. For example, while the Will is rushing to the right to pursue the run, what the play is actually doing is bringing the linebacker closer to his assigned blockers.

Julian Edelman starts in quick motion coming across the formation with Sherman matching him step-for-step. At the snap, Brady opens up and gives a token fake to Edelman and then continues backward to the mesh point with Blount.

The structure of the formation is such that the defense is essentially boxed in, with the single high safety look meaning that the Seahawk defense is packed tight in the tackle box, and the Patriots are testing the reaction to the jet sweep fake. In this case Chancellor at the FS spot does take a couple steps and flow in the direction of the jet sweep, but closer to the line of scrimmage, Earl Thomas has to work hard to avoid getting himself blocked by Brandon LaFell, whose tight split to his side allows him a chance to pin the edge defenders inside, and the press coverage means he'll have an easier time blocking two people at once.

Meanwhile, at the point of attack, the 3 technique defensive tackle splits the double team and forces Blount to cut wider, where the TE is outnumbered 2 to 1, and Blount has to just get vertical and settle for whatever he can.

Still, the Patriots pick up two yards and gain more information on their opponent to put away for future use later on in the game.

New England Drive 1 / Play 6 / 3ʳᵈ & 6 / -35 Yard Line / Left Hash / 12:15 1Q
NE – 0 SEA – 0

Summary
Pass intended for Shane Vereen out to the left is incomplete

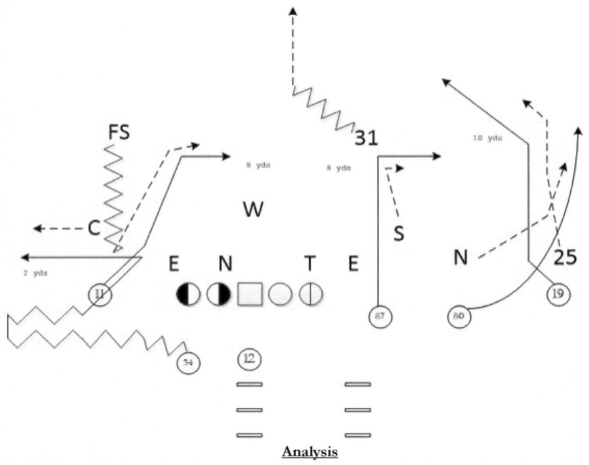

Analysis

Once again the Patriots line up with a tight split from the X receiver, then motion the back out of the backfield and splits him out wide. This is one of the many ways that the Patriot offense has to get a read on their opponents.

The entire goal of sending Vereen out wide to the left was not only to see who followed him, but also to see if the defense would leave the short middle area of the field undefended. "Who cares as long as the deep passes are taken care of," you might ask. "Isn't the whole idea to back off, force a throw underneath, then rally to the ball to make their tackle?"

There are definitely situations where that's true, but the New England offense is very skilled at shallow crossing concepts that attack the underneath middle of the field. Not only do they have the necessary tools in their playbook to take advantage of an open middle, but they also happen to have several speedy guys, including Vereen, who can make the catch and turn the corner on whoever covers up to make the tackle. In this case, the guys in the Seattle secondary adjust, with the FS coming down to press Edelman, and the corner widening to take Vereen.

Once the defense has finished moving around, Brady surveys the middle of the field and makes the final check at the line. The linebacker playing in the middle of the box is still sitting there in his original position. For this reason, Brady changes the routes of Edelman and Vereen to attack the weak spots of the defense which is away from the underneath middle.

Vereen's route is changed to a 'whip' route which acts as if he heading underneath on a shallow crossing route, but instead whips back outside. The pass is a little too wide, however and it falls incomplete.

New England Punt

PRO PUNT 53 STACK

Seattle Punt Return

53 STACK   8 MAN BLOCK

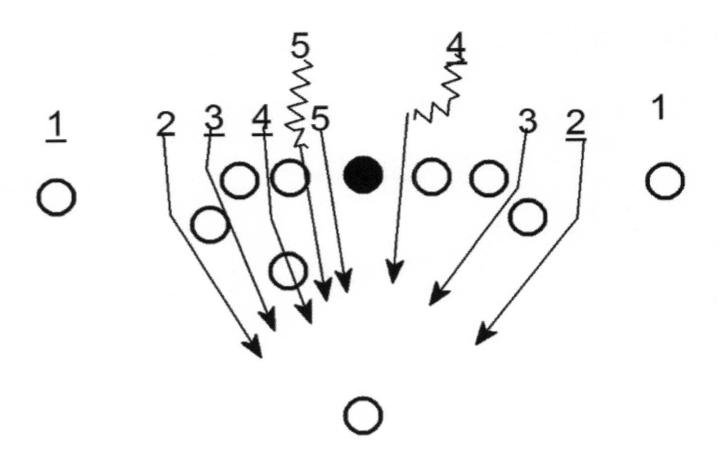

NEW ENGLAND DRIVE #1 REVIEW

Early on, the Patriots offense has shown Seattle several different formations, motions, and personnel groups.

One of their objectives in moving so many people around early on is to find out how the secondary and the defensive front will react to different motions.

In the case of the Z receiver, the corner (Sherman) is responsible for chasing the receiver across the formation stride-for-stride. Seattle is well aware of New England's fondness for handing the football off to the receiver in motion on the jet sweep, so it makes sense that they would make sure that there is a defender assigned to follow the receiver in motion wherever he goes. It's worth noting that this rule only applies to the #1 or widest receiver in the formation. In the cases of slot receivers, like on the first play of the game when Edelman goes in motion from left to right, the defense reacts by bumping out the linebacker to the opposite side of the formation.

Likewise, Gronkowski has already been moved around to just about every position on the field, and the Seattle defense has been forced to account for him since he had the football thrown his way on the first play of the game.

The fake jet sweep by New England is a great example of how Seattle is in danger of getting outflanked to the single receiver side of the formation, especially when that receiver is lined up in a tight split. The press coverage that Seattle is playing to that side makes it easier in some ways for a skilled receiver like Brandon LaFell to gain the edge, not to mention that Kam Chancellor in the free safety position on this play is aligned so far to the right side that an adjustment is needed in order to properly play against the jet sweep.

Shane Vereen will have his opportunities in the flat as well, especially coming underneath the vertical release of Gronkowski to the single receiver side.

Seattle Drive 1 / Play 1 / 1ˢᵗ & 10 / -16 Yard Line / Right Hash / 11:34 1Q

NE – 0 SEA – 0

Summary

Gain of 3 yards by Marshawn Lynch along the right side.

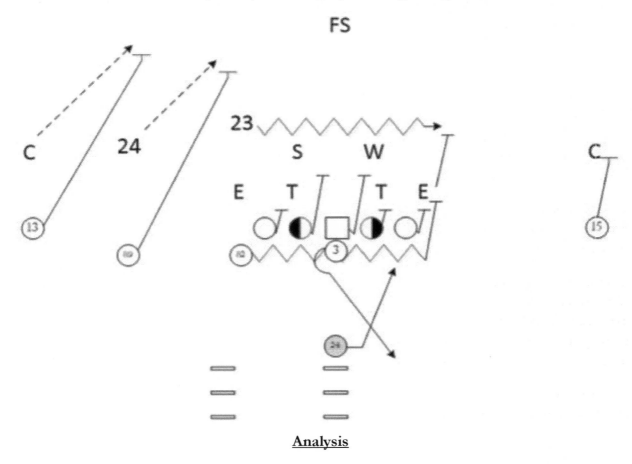

Analysis

Revis is lined up across from Doug Baldwin, and since he's lined up in the slot, it gives Seattle's coaches an idea of how New England will play Baldwin.

The combo block to the front side of the play on the 3 technique turns out not to be a combo at all, since because of the wide alignment and movement of the defensive tackle and the Will linebacker, the center has a free release and lazy path to the 2nd level so that he can get a block on the Will.

They send Luke Wilson from right to left which brings the down safety Patrick Chung with him. This flips the strength of the formation from left to right, but the structure of the Patriot defense doesn't change inside the tackle box.

Seattle Drive 1 / Play 2 / 2nd & 7 / -19 Yard Line / Right Hash / 11:15 1Q
NE – 0 SEA - 0

Summary

Gain of 5 yards on the carry by Marshawn Lynch

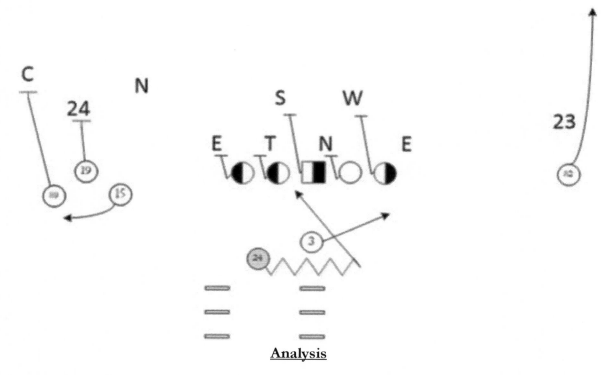

Analysis

This time Seattle lines up the tight end Luke Wilson out wide to the right where he's covered by Patrick Chung. Meanwhile the offense flips Marshawn Lynch from left to right and the ball is snapped so fast that Wilfork at the nose doesn't have a chance to readjust and bump over, leaving the right DE Rob Ninkovich playing up the field and giving too much room to the inside which gives Lynch the room he needs to hit a crease inside the tackles.

To the opposite side of the formation there are 3 receivers lined up in a bunch set and Seattle's coaches get a good look at how the Patriots will defend this bunch look. Revis lines up over the point of the bunch, and presses Douglas McNeil #19 as he's coming off the line of scrimmage, with a good amount of cushion being played by the corners to either side.

Seattle Drive 1 / Play 3 / 3rd & 2 / -24 Yard Line / Right Hash / 10:32 1Q
NE – 0 SEA – 0

Summary

No gain on the carry for Marshawn Lynch up the middle.

Analysis

This play is blown up on the backside by Vince Wilfork, who beats the block from the RT trying to cut him off from the play. It's hard enough to block a guy like Wilfork straight up, but if you're not able to get your head across and turn your body so that your butt is in between him and the gap you're trying to protect where all your weight is, he's bringing his entire body with him, and you're hoping that you're gonna be able to stop him based on pure arm strength.

He's so quick off the ball that you line him up in a 3 technique and still have him able to chase down a play from behind. If you're running a play away from him, you'd better be able to hit the hole quickly to the front side of the play, otherwise he'll get free and chase you down. If you're running right at him, you'd better double team him, because very few offensive linemen in the NFL are good enough to block Wilfork one-on-one. If you double him, that means you've got 3 linemen left for five defenders in the box (assuming no TE), and someone is gonna get to the ball carrier.

Seattle Punt

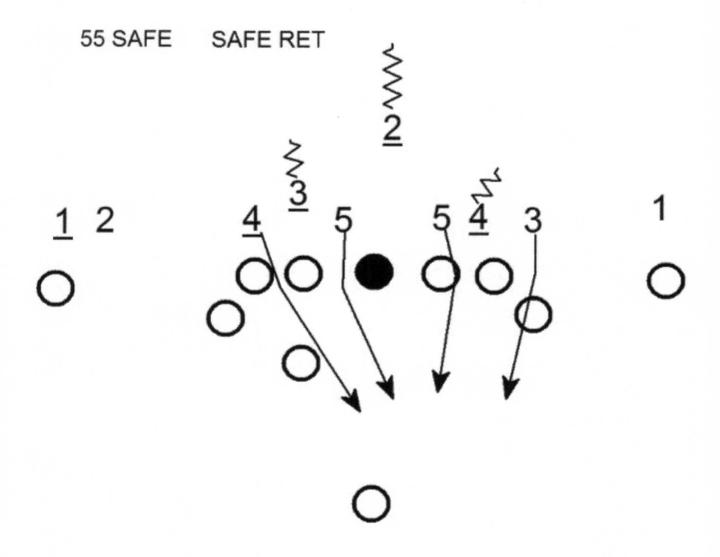

55 SAFE   SAFE RET

New England Punt Return

PRO PUNT 55 SAFE

SEATTLE DRIVE #1 REVIEW

The Seahawks want to get an idea of what defensive fronts to expect from New England early on, as well as how they can influence the defenders on the edge.

A couple of questions Seattle needs to answer include how are the Patriots going to treat their "Y-off" formation, especially out of the gun, (since there are so many more threats when the TE is off the line of scrimmage in the shotgun), as well as how they're going to deal with "change of strength" motion, and what effect, if any, is flipping Lynch back and forth going to have.

In this respect, having a guy like Lynch who can get downhill and get yardage against most defenses is a huge help, because he allows offensive coordinator Darrell Bevell to mess around with formations, and move guys around on offense without having to worry that the offense has to get a perfect look from the defense in order to be able to run the football. Having a numbers advantage in the box, to one side of the formation or the other is nice, but when you've got a guy like Lynch, who usually requires more than one defender to bring down, you have the ability to run plays that might not look very promising on paper.

For an offensive coach, Lynch is basically the offensive equivalent of a 2-gap defensive lineman, a guy who can give you a numbers advantage all by himself. Speaking of two-gap players on defense, the Patriots have two very good ones on the field to start the game, #75 Vince Wilfork and #96 Sealver Siliga, the two defensive tackles in the 4-2 nickel package that New England starts the game with.

On 2nd down, Wilfork was aligned in a 1-technique on the nose to the right side, but Seattle flopped Lynch to the opposite side and snapped the ball before the defense had time to adjust, creating a huge gap to the right side and lots of space to run through.

This is something that New England will have to figure out as the game goes on. As long as they set the defensive front to one side or the other, they'll be in danger of getting "out-flanked" instantly if Seattle decide to flip the single back in the backfield when they're in the gun, as quickly and casually as they did twice on the opening drive.

The question Bill Belichick has to answer is this: How do we play a defensive front that allows us to use our preferred method of two-gap defensive tackles while still staying sound to both sides.

The answer, at least when it comes to the nickel package that New England starts out in, may be lining up in a balanced front where flipping the back doesn't give the offense much of a strategic advantage.

New England Drive 2 / Play 1 / 1ˢᵗ & 10 / -32 Yard Line / Middle / 9:20 1Q

NE – 0 SEA – 0

Summary

Screen pass to Vereen out of the backfield for a gain of three yards.

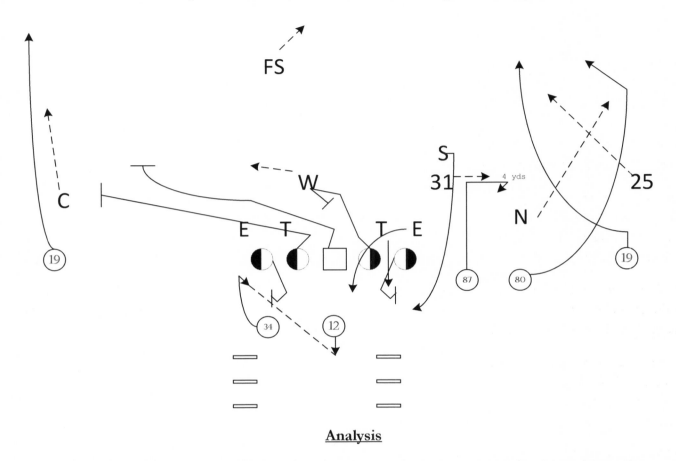

Analysis

After seeing the alignment of the defense against this formation on the previous drive, the Patriots come back to it. Because they have a pretty good idea that Kam Chancellor and Richard Sherman will both be on the same side of the formation, the screen play to Vereen to the other side is a great way to keep the football away from two of their best defenders.

As an added bonus, the Sam linebacker KJ Wright blitzes off the right edge, meaning that Bobby Wagner at the Will backer spot is the only 2nd-level guy inside the box they have to worry about.

Wagner does an excellent job of diagnosing the play, but also puts himself in a good position by starting to widen out at the snap since he knows the defense is vulnerable to the single receiver side. By widening out, he forces the play back inside to the defensive linemen who have retraced their steps and found Vereen.

New England Drive 2 / Play 2 / 2nd & 7 / -35 Yard Line / Left Hash / 9:03 1Q

NE – 0 SEA – 0

Summary

Pass out to the left complete to Edelman for a gain of eleven yards and a first down.

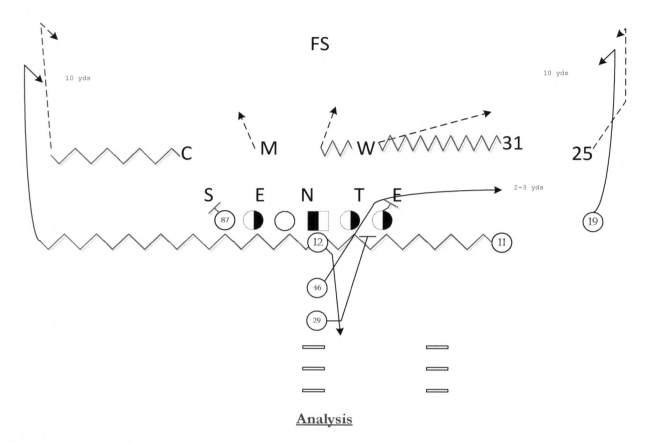

Analysis

The Patriots go back to the Twins formation and the defense gives them pretty much the same look as last time, with Sherman and Chancellor both lined up to the twins side.

This time they send the slot receiver in motion from right to left to get a read on the reaction of the defense, and predictability Chancellor stays to the right and Byron Maxwell the opposite corner, ends up widening with the motion and playing the deep third to that side.

Seattle is playing with the Bruce Irvin up near the line and on the outside shoulder of Gronk. At the snap, Brady carries out the play fake, and Gronk fires out in the same way he would on a run play. Irvin was already playing pretty aggressively, but with the backfield action and the acting job from Gronk, he's not in position to undercut the route by Edelman.

Seattle Drive 2 / Play 3 / 1ˢᵗ & 10 / -46 Yard Line / Left Hash / 8:31 1Q
NE – 0 SEA – 0

Summary
Gain of six up the middle by Blount

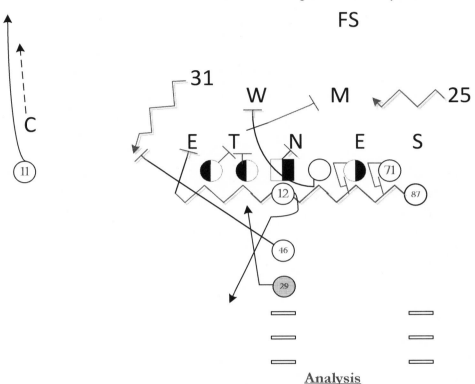

Analysis

New England stays in the I formation but brings on an offensive tackle as an extra tight end. For the first time in the game, the Patriots come out in 22 personnel, and Seattle doesn't change their personnel group on the field because they've already got five defensive linemen out there, albeit one of them being Irvin who is more of a DE/OLB-type player.

The defense stays in an "under" look with the Sam linebacker up on the line to the TE strength and Chancellor aligned to the pass strength. As Gronk goes in motion, Sherman makes sure the strong DE bumps over to slant toward the play from the backside.

Plays like this are why Blount is on the field to begin with. He hits the A gap hard and gets the offense way ahead of the count on 1st down.

One can't help but wonder, if Seattle is going to play 21 personnel the same way they play 22 personnel, why you wouldn't just get back in 22 personnel when you want to run the football out of the I-formation. In other words, they're going to have five defensive linemen on the field no matter what, so why not put an extra big guy of your own out there to win at the line of scrimmage.

New England Drive 2 / Play 4 / 2ⁿᵈ & 4 / +48 Yard Line / Left Hash / 7:46 1Q
NE – 0 SEA – 0

Summary

Gain of one yard by Blount on the run to the right side.

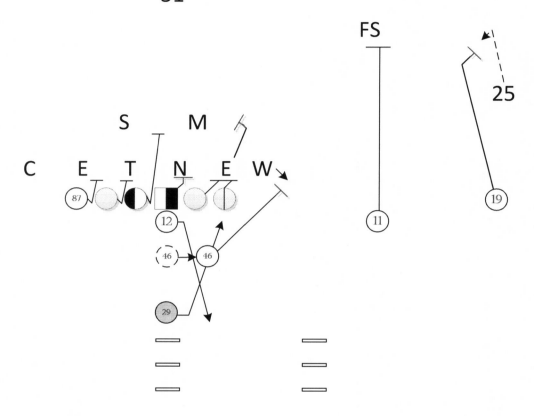

Analysis

This is another example of Brady using audibles at the line of scrimmage.

Seattle has curiously decided to flip their strength call since the last time New England lined up in twins two plays earlier. This time Irvin lines up to the open side of the formation, away from the tight end Gronkowski, and Brady moves the fullback to an offset position to the right so he's in a better position to kick out Irvin.

New England may be hesitant to run to Gronkowski's side in this outside zone scheme, or they may just like the angle on the play side combo between the right guard and right tackle moving up to the Mike linebacker better than the situation to the left, but either way, this play doesn't go for much at all.

New England Drive 2 / Play 5 / 3rd & 3 / +47 Yard Line / Right Hash / 7:06 1Q
NE – 0 SEA – 0

Summary

Pass complete to Gronkowski on the hitch screen to the right, he picks up four yards and the first down.

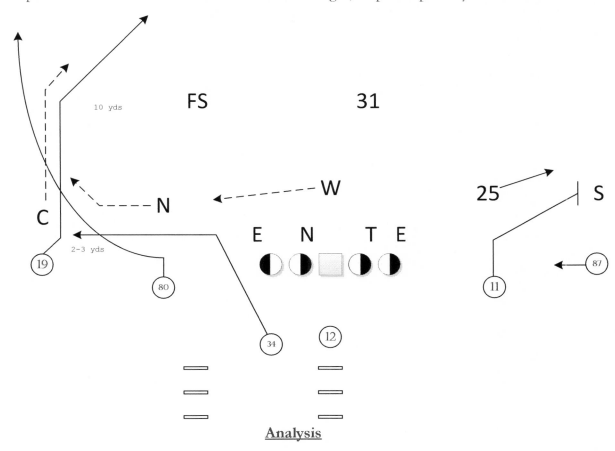

Analysis

Even though this is categorized as a "hitch screen" to Gronk, there really is no hitch route involved, nor even an attempt at giving the appearance at getting vertical. Instead, Gronk turns inside right away, running perfectly down the line of scrimmage, with Edelman ear-holing the linebacker KJ Wright whom the Seahawks have lined up over Gronkowski.

Meanwhile Richard Sherman follows the movement of Edelman on the kick out block, which opens a crease just big enough for Gronk to pick up some momentum and get past the sticks. This is one of the many ways the Patriots have to get the ball in the hands of their incredibly talented TE, and given Brady's accuracy and Gronk's size and power, this isn't much different than handing the ball to a hulking fullback on 3rd and short and asking him to pick up the 1st down, only instead of having to put his head down and grind it out against the big guys in the middle of the defense, this play leaves him one on one with a guy a lot smaller and lighter than he is. It basically assures that he'll be matched up with Sherman, whether the defense likes it or not.

New England Drive 2 / Play 6 / 1ˢᵗ & 10 / +43 / Right Hash / 6:28 1Q
NE – 0 SEA – 0

Summary

Completion to Vereen out of the backfield on the left for a gain of three yards.

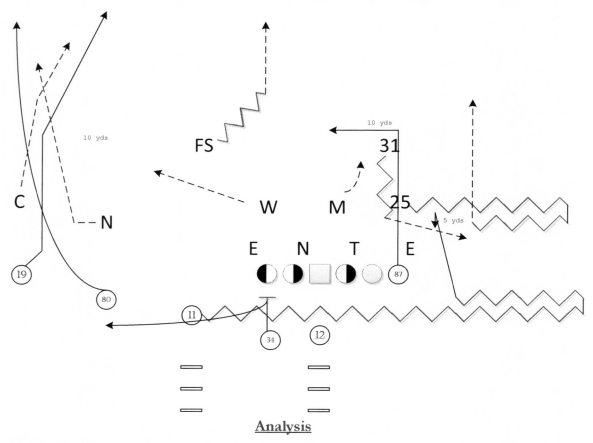

Analysis

Brady peeks over at the TE side of the formation after taking the snap, and sees the combination of Chancellor and Wagner squeezing the area of the TE and Z receiver's routes. He's looking to get the football to Edelman right away, but since he feels the pass rush getting closer and decides to dump it off to Vereen on the check-release swing route.

The deep drop off of all the defenders to that side of the formation gives him lots of space to operate once he has the ball in his hands, but credit the recovery speed of this defense and their ability to fly to the football. It's what's made them such a dangerous defense all season long.

Still, if New England can get that kind of open space for Vereen to work with, they'll take it, especially if the next time he's running a flat route instead of a flare, and getting toward the line of scrimmage more quickly.

New England Drive 2 / Play 7 / 2ⁿᵈ & 7 / +40 Yard Line / Left Hash / 5:51 1Q
NE – 0 SEA – 0

Summary

Gain of six yards up the middle

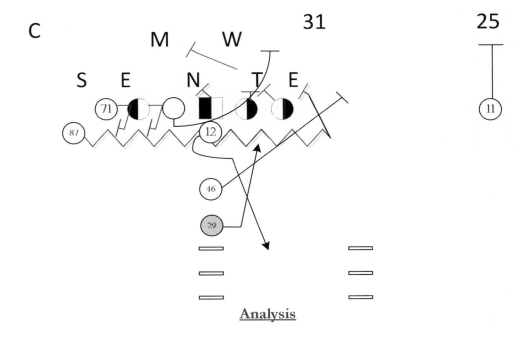

Analysis

Seattle is getting better at disrupting the play from the backside, as this play shows.

When Gronkowski crosses the formation in motion, the Sam linebacker Irvin taps the left DE Michael Taylor on the shoulder and gets him to slant inside to the B gap, and Taylor's penetration into the backfield nearly creates a problem by almost getting a hand on Blount in the backfield as he's picking up steam.

This I Formation Wing alignment with Gronkowski having the ability to go in motion is the formation they've put into the game plan with the expressed purpose of running the football away from Fleming's side.

New England Drive 2 / Play 8 / 3rd & 1 / +34 Yard Line / Left Hash / 5:13 1Q
NE – 0 SEA – 0

Summary
Gain of eight on the run by Blount around the right side and the first down.

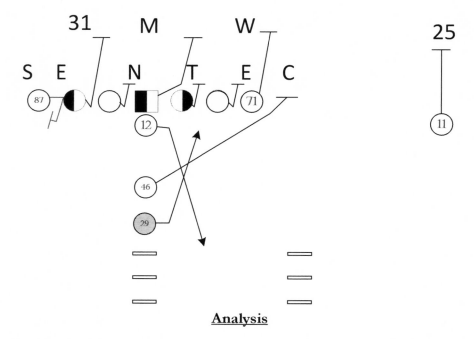

Analysis

These are very smart splits by the New England offensive line, and this time New England runs the wide zone right at Maxwell playing the edge, and away from Kam Chancellor, who is down in the box against this formation. More importantly, however, they are running the play away from the nose tackle, which means that the offensive line can get double team blocks on the three technique and the seven technique to the play side, since they've got such good angles.

The matchup with Develin blocking out on the corner Byron Maxwell to the strong side is very advantageous for the New England and plays a big part in the success of this particular play.

Seattle's defense needs to make an adjustment to their alignment against this formation or else they risk getting outflanked for the rest of the game, especially in crucial situations, since New England is likely going to rely on this set when they need a single yard the most.

New England Drive 2 / Play 9 / 1ˢᵗ & 10 / +26 Yard Line / Right Hash / 4:33 1Q
NE – 0 SEA – 0

Summary
Gain of two yards up the middle by Blount

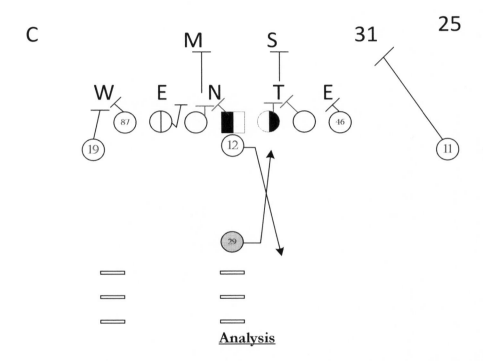

Analysis

Here's where New England lines up in a compressed formation to one side and a normal split to the other. Interesting to note that New England puts "regular" personnel on the field but provides an 8-man surface to the defense, meaning that Chancellor is playing in a halfway position in the right alley.

Once again, the Patriots hand off the ball to Blount heading the opposite direction as the offensive line. As was discussed earlier, part of this is to set up a natural cutback lane, but also to bring the linebackers closer to the linemen coming off of their combo blocks.

This play also allows New England to observe how the defense, especially in this particular under front, will play against a compressed look to either side of the formation.

New England Drive 2 / Play 10 / 2ⁿᵈ & 8 / +24 Yard Line / Right Hash / 4:02 1Q
NE – 0 SEA – 0

Summary
Pass complete to Amendola to the left for a gain of ten yards and a first down.

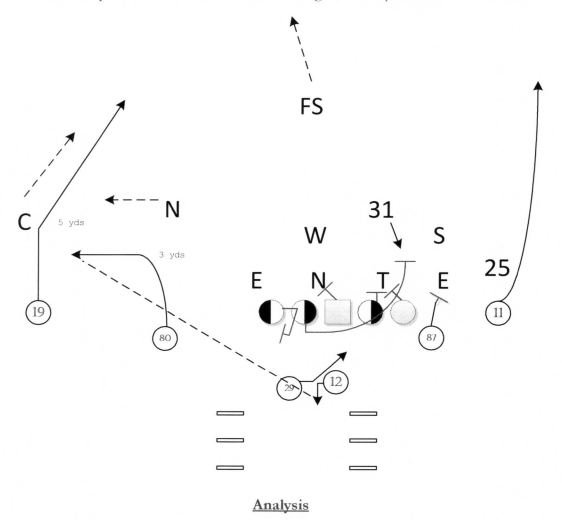

Analysis

The play-fake by Brady to Blount manages to hold the nickel corner and opens up a lot of space outside the numbers for Amendola to make the catch and pick up the first down.

This is another example of how important details and precision are in the passing game, especially as it relates to the timing of the pass. The 3-yard depth of the out route by Amendola is timed up to break just as Brady in carrying out the fake, which forces the defender, at the very least, to stay in one place, which is only slightly better than biting completely on the fake and running toward the backfield.

Remember, the first goal of these concepts is to cause the defensive player to hesitate.

The corner, Maxwell, defending LaFell, vacates the area outside by following the slant route and opens the door for Amendola to make the catch and turn up the field for the first down.

New England Drive 2 / Play 11 /1ˢᵗ & 10 / +14 Yard Line / Left Hash / 3:30 1Q
NE – 0 SEA – 0

Summary

Completion to Hoomanawanui on the hitch route to the right side for a gain of four yards.

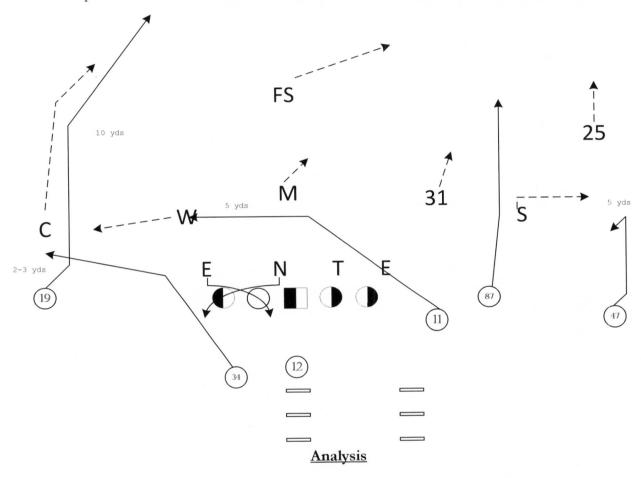

Analysis

The Patriots continue to play formation games with Seattle, splitting Gronk and Hoomanawanui out to the far right side to see how the defense reacts. Naturally the defense is very concerned whenever Gronk is split out wide like this, and so they align accordingly, with Sherman giving Hoomanawanui a large cushion in order to play over the top of any vertical out-breaking routes by Gronk, like in a smash concept.

Meanwhile the post-cross-flat route to the opposite side of the formation are designed to take advantage of any extra attention to Gronk and Hoomanawanui, especially the FS, whose position on the field is replaced by the post route by LaFell. Then once Edelman gets past the Mike linebacker he should have a nice opportunity to get open.

New England Drive 2 / Play 12 / 2nd & 6 / +10 Yard Line / Right Hash / 2:52 1Q
NE – 0 SEA – 0

Summary
No gain on the run up the middle by Blount

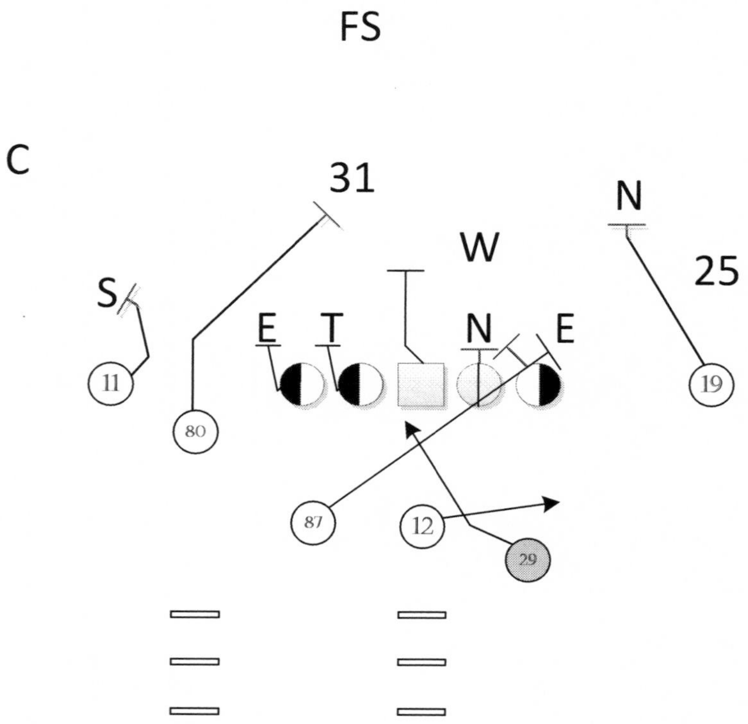

FS

C

31

N

W

25

S

E   T   N   E

11

80

19

87   12

29

Analysis

Cliff Avril #56 is the backside DE and does a great job avoiding Gronk's sloppy attempt at the kick out block on the backside of the inside zone play, but that's not even the worst block on the this side of the offensive line. At the snap, the right guard gets beat by the 3 technique into the backfield who ends up making the tackle.

In theory, the tackle and guard should be working together on this play, but the DT squares up the guard, meaning that the RT's path to the 2nd-level is completely clean, so he heads up to the Will linebacker.

New England Drive 2 / Play 13 / 3rd & 6 / +10 Yard Line / Right Hash / 2:16 1Q

NE – 0 SEA – 0

Summary

Pass intended for Edelman is intercepted by Jeremy Lane

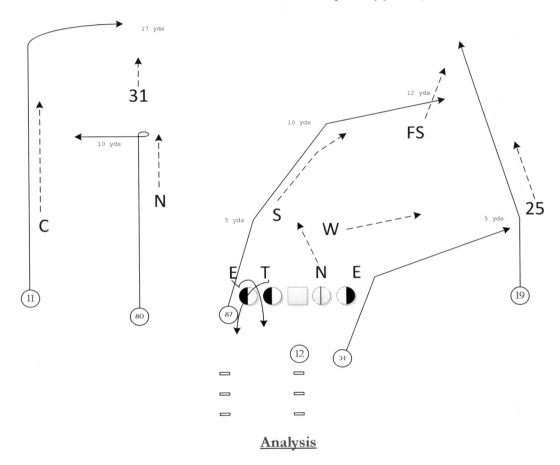

Analysis

This is a brilliant job by the Seattle defensive line to create pressure with only 3 pass rushers against five offensive linemen. Since the nose tackle engages for a split-second before dropping into the short zone, the middle three offensive linemen and end up freeing up the defensive ends on either side one-on-one situations against the offensive tackles. Then the 3 technique stunts all the way around and nearly sacks Tom Brady as he releases the football.

Meanwhile back in the secondary, the Patriots are trying to stretch the field horizontally, but since the offense is on the 10 yard line, they don't have the room to run the same concepts that they could in the open field. The reason being is that with Amendola making his cut at the goal line, the window is very tight between the nickel inside of him and the corner to the outside.

The corner is playing a 4-deep technique to his side, which means he's keeping one eye on the slot receiver in case he makes a cut to the outside, and he'll then pass the vertical route of #1 off to the safety.

Even for Brady, this is a really tight window to get the ball into, and when he's hurried and trying to get the ball to Edelman in the back of the end zone, the nickel Jeremy Lane is there to intercept it.

NEW ENGLAND DRIVE #2 REVIEW

One way to get the ball to the right side of the field is to line up a tight end at the #1 receiver position out wide and throw a hitch. Sherman isn't going to press the tight end, since there's no reason to. Gronk is bigger than him and he doesn't have the burst off the line that could challenge Sherman deep. There's also the fact that he doesn't want to create a void in the space behind him for a smash concept to develop. Seattle isn't worried about yards after the catch either, since they're great at rallying to the ball and gang tackling the ball carrier. The attention being paid to Vereen is also paying dividends, as the coverage to the weak side is very quick to vacate to the weak side is very quick to vacate the underneath middle when they see Vereen running out to the flat.

One of the big points of emphasis coming into the game for New England was how to create opportunities for Edelman and Amendola over the middle. You can call all the shallow crossing routes you want, but you're basically wasting your receivers if you're sending them over the middle to get knocked around by the defenders playing coverage.

There's also the issue of the 22 personnel package that New England is rolling out on this drive. The key is that the two formations the Patriots are lining up in out of this personnel group presents very different challenges for the defense. The idea is that you throw the same guys out onto the field, but as a defensive coordinator you have no idea what kind of look you're getting.

One look is better for running a power scheme, the other is better for running a power scheme, the other is better for running more to the edge, so Dan Quinn needs to coach his guys up on formation recognition and where they fit, especially the edge defenders, because Seattle can't afford to keep having their corner have to take on a fullback on the edge like on play #8 of the drive.

Brady got greedy on that final play, and Seattle did a tremendous job of taking away all the deep throws, and Brady had his eyes locked into one side of the field and tried to get away with a very risky throw. As a result he basically takes 3 points off the board for his team, and Seattle comes off the field with a huge victory in this situation.

Seattle Drive 2 / Play 1 / 1ˢᵗ & 10 / -14 Yard Line / Right Hash / 1:39 1Q

NE – 0 SEA – 0

Summary

Gain of 7 yards on Russell Wilson's scramble off of the boot play.

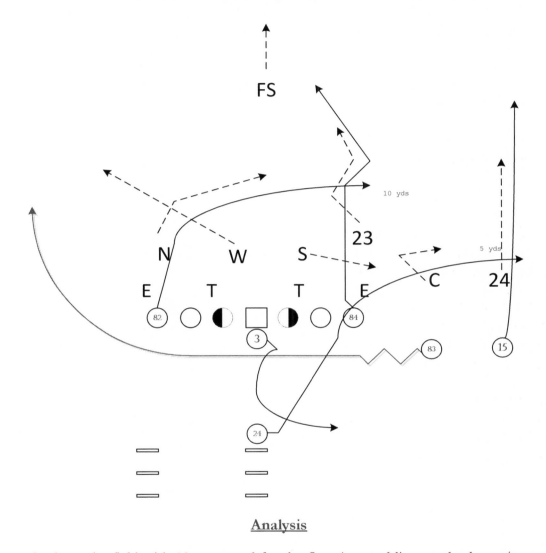

Analysis

Seattle comes back on the field with 12 personnel for the first time and lines up both receivers to the same side.

Bringing Ricardo Lockette in jet motion to a position where Wilson opens up to fake the jet sweep to the left before sprinting to the right while Lockette continues on his path before turning it into a wheel route where he turns up the field around the numbers on the left side of the field.

Initially Wilson eyes the flat route by Lynch, which is covered by the corner #25 Kyle Arrington and the Sam linebacker #91 Jamie Collins. As the unblocked DE Rob Ninkovich comes up the field and gets close to Wilson, Wilson peeks back at Lockette running the wheel route but doesn't have time to reset his body and throwback to the opposite side of the field. This could've been avoided by having Lynch "chip" on

Ninkovich as he leaves the flat, since he's not the primary target on this play anyway. Wilson tucks the ball, jukes Ninkovich, and manages to pick up 7 yards by running down the field.

Wilson's read before the snap relies on watching if the defense brings anyone in motion along with Lockette on the jet sweep motion, and since they don't, Wilson knows it's almost certain that the wheel route will be wide open because the nickel defender to that side should be taking the drag route by Wilson, and leaving Lockette all alone to the left side of the field.

Also of note is the route by Cooper Helfet #84, who initially looks as though he's running the corner route to complete a flood concept to that side, but just after breaking to the corner at the 10 yard mark, he'll break back in toward the post and if the FS leaves the middle of the field to chase the wheel route, then Helfet's route should be wide open.

Wilson still manages to set up a great situation for 2nd down, but if he had just a couple moments longer Seattle could've found themselves on the opposite side of the 50 in a hurry.

Seattle Drive 2 / Play 2 / 2nd & 3 / -21 Yard Line / Right Hash / 1:17 1Q

NE – 0 SEA - 0

Summary

Gain of 4 yards by Marshawn Lynch on the carry to the left side.

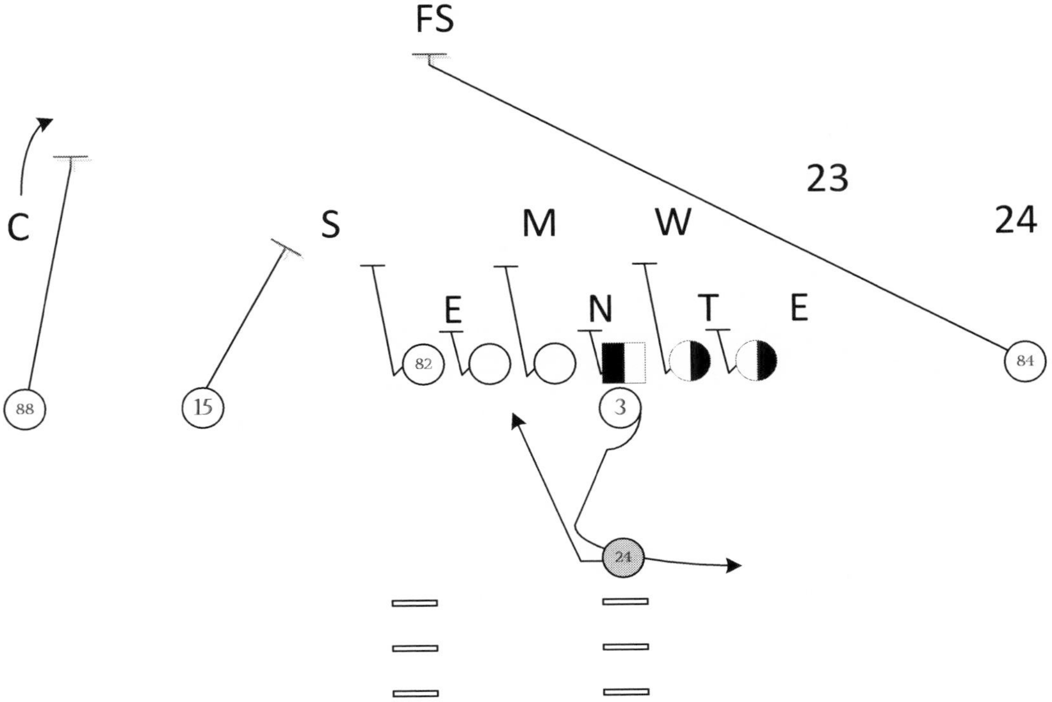

Analysis

The Seahawks go to 13 personnel, splitting out Helfet wide to the right as the single receiver with and Wilson as the attached TE to the three receiver side, then to the far left we see Tony Moeaki split out wide to the left of Jermain Kearse.

Belichick decides to bring some extra size on to the field to deal with this three TE personnel package Seattle is playing with, bringing on #55 Akeem Ayers as an extra linebacker who is the Sam in the diagram above and splitting the difference between Jermaine Kearse and Luke Wilson. Meanwhile Patrick Chung lines up to the opposite side, in the alley to the single receiver side of the formation. This gives them an alley/edge player to the both sides of the formation. McCourty the FS aligns himself on the left hash, over the top of Wilson the TE. New England lines up in an "under" front, expecting a compressed formation, but Seattle lines up in this 3x1 set.

Seattle has a personnel advantage in the passing game to the 3 receiver side, since Kearse is lined up across from a linebacker, but they run the wide zone out to the left. On the backside, the offensive line cuts Wilfork and Collins to eliminate the threat of the backside pursuit.

Lynch cuts up inside of the left tackle and manages to pick up the 1st down.

Seattle Drive 2 / Play 3 / 1ˢᵗ & 10 / -25 Yard Line / Left Hash / 0:35 1Q

NE – 0 SEA – 0

Summary

Sack! Russell Wilson sacked by Darrelle Revis for a loss of 2 yards on the scramble to the left side.

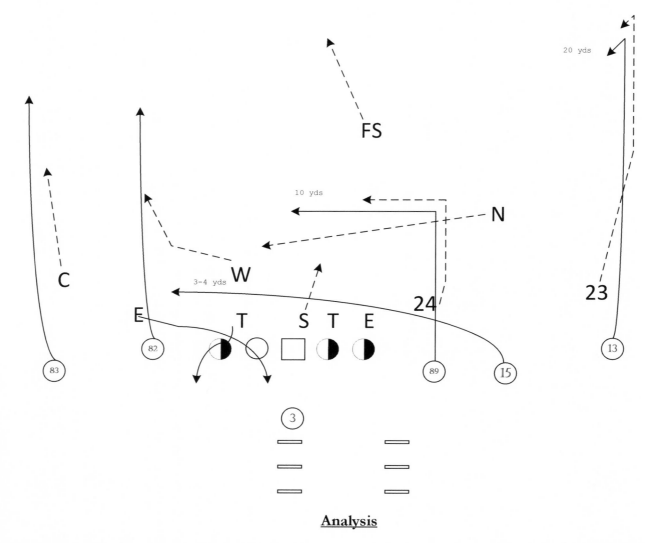

Analysis

Wilson hesitates far too long on this throw. He has all kinds of time to survey the field. Even though Donta Hightower at the Sam spot drops into the path of the drive route by Kearse, he doesn't actually disrupt the route, so Wilson can easily get him the football as soon as he crosses the left hash and can even get it to Baldwin coming in behind on the dig route at 10 yards. For some reason he still holds out for something else, and is eventually flushed out of the pocket and sacked.

Seattle Drive 2 / Play 4 / 2nd & 12 / -23 Yard Line / Left Hash / 15:00 2Q

NE – 0 SEA – 0

Summary

Gain of 3 yards on the carry to the right side by Marshawn Lynch

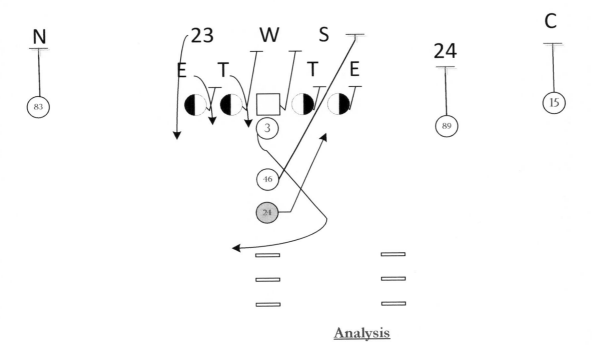

Analysis

Given the long-yardage situation on 2nd and 12, New England opts to leave their speedy nickel personnel on the field, even as Seattle brings in a fullback.

It's another wide zone scheme that Seattle has already run in this game, and the Seahawks, now behind schedule, are attempting to get to a 3rd and manageable situation by running the ball.

Vince Wilfork is a factor once again, holding up the right guard at the line of scrimmage before disengaging and bringing down Marshawn Lynch after a short gain. Donta Hightower takes on the fullback, but if the right guard for Seattle can manage to get his head across and win his inside gap, it could've turned into a whole lot more.

Seattle Drive 2 / Play 5 / 3ʳᵈ & 9 / -26 Yard Line / Right Hash / 14:45 2Q

NE – 0 SEA – 0

Summary

Pass incomplete intended for Douglass McNeil over the middle.

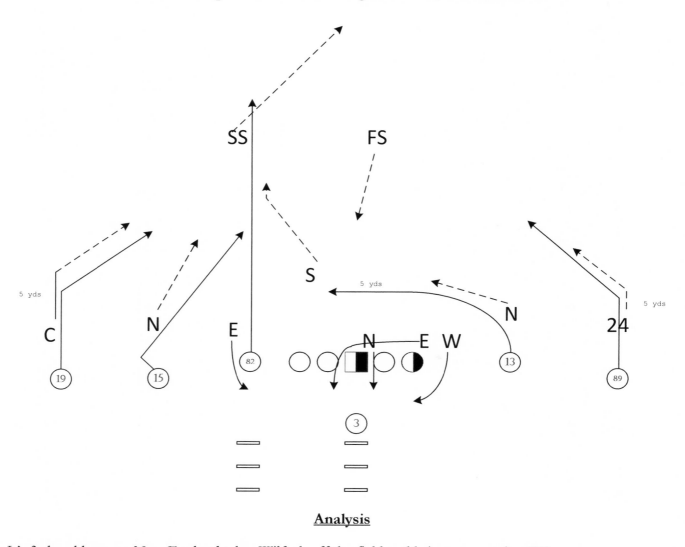

Analysis

It's 3rd and long, so New England takes Wilfork off the field and brings on another DB.

New England starts off in a 2-deep shell with Devin McCourty rotating down underneath as a robber safety to take away any routes in the middle of the field.

At the snap, Wilson looks to his left at McNeil #19, who is about to break inside on a slant route, but just as he's about to break open, Wilson starts feeling the heat and he has to scramble around. He manages to keep his eyes downfield and heaves up a pass for McNeil who is streaking down the middle of the field, but the ball is overthrown and Seattle has to punt.

Seattle Punt

PRO PUNT 55 SAFE

New England Punt Return

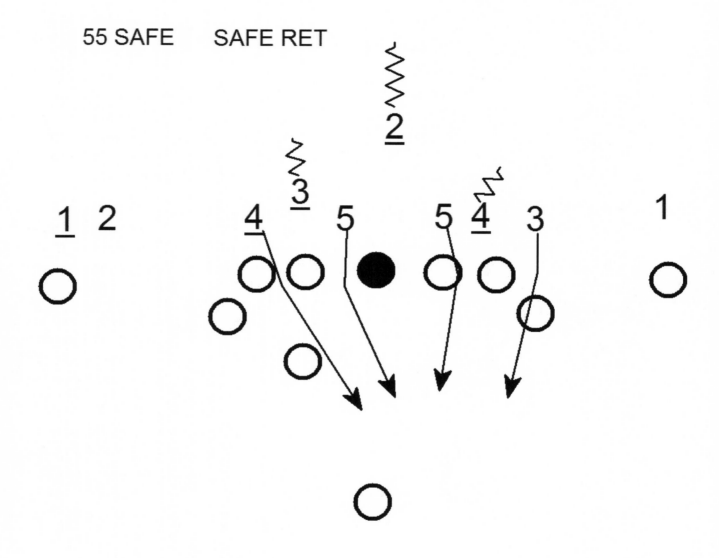

SEATTLE DRIVE #2 REVIEW

In five plays, the Seahawks come out with four different personnel groupings, as well as giving the New England defense a few different formations and backfield sets to worry about. Now we're to the next phase of the Darrell Bevell's game plan. On the first play of the drive, Seattle brings on a 2nd TE on the field for the 1st time, but New England remains in their nickel personnel on defense.

Bevell was hoping to force the Patriots to bring on an extra linebacker, then go for the big play on a complicated trick play that should take advantage of the personnel on the field. However, when that doesn't work, and the Patriots keep the same personnel on the field, he brings on a 3rd TE, meaning that now Seattle has 1 RB, 3 TEs and 1 WR on the field, which finally forces New England to bring on an extra linebacker.

However, even with the 3rd TE on the field, Bevell still doesn't exactly do what's expected. Instead of lining up in a compressed formation the offense aligns themselves in a more conventional-looking 3x1 set, which forces the Sam linebacker to play out in space between #2 and #3 to the right, and opening up running room off-tackle. They've also found another way to "pick-a-side" and run to the open B gap, similar to the way the offense kept flipping the back on the last drive to find the best side to run the football.

Also of note is the fact that the SS Patrick Chung is aligned to #84 Helfet's side, since when multiple TEs are on the field for Seattle, and for a lot of teams actually, they'll line up their 2nd TE to the pass strength in order to create opportunities for the #1 TE in the pass game, and also usually because they can get the defense to set their numbers to the pass strength while still having an advantage in the run game to the single receiver side.

This allows offensive coaches like Bevell to play formation games with the defense, and to a large part pick and choose where he wants the SS to line up. It's also worth mentioning that when you've got 3 TEs on the field, at least one of them will be off the ball, opening up the possibility of gap schemes, like the counter play for example, or any kind of play where the "off" TE will cross the formation on a pull up to the second level or on a path to "wham" the end man on the line of scrimmage to the opposite side.

In the pass game, Belichick has decided to crowd the middle of the field to make it tougher on Wilson and take away the easy throws over the middle, allowing the defenders in pass coverage to win their individual matchups at each position. New England brought Dime personnel onto the field on 3rd and long and after starting a 2-deep look pre-snap, the free safety rotated to a single-high look to take away the middle of the field. So far, it's working, as on both pass plays Wilson has been forced to scramble around without any success.

New England Drive 3 / Play 1 / 1st & 10 / -35 Yard Line / Right Hash / 13:57 2Q

NE – 0 SEA – 0

Summary

Pass completed to Amendola on the receiver screen to the left side for a gain of 17 yards and a first down.

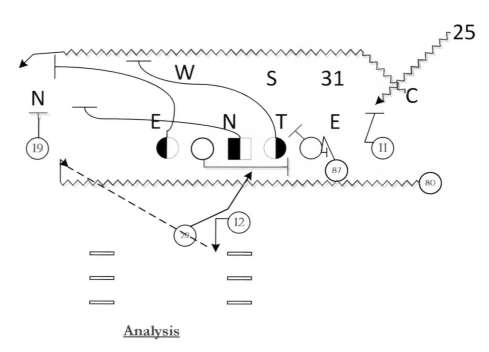

Analysis

The Patriots continue to find ways to manufacture high-percentage plays out of the shotgun, and this time it's Amendola with the ball in his hands making things happen. It's only because of the pursuit by Earl Thomas, the FS, that this play doesn't go for a touchdown. He originally forces Amendola outside from the alley, but also avoids getting caught up in the mess of blockers and defenders at the point of attack. Using speed and proper angles, he forces Amendola out of bounds after a 17-yard gain.

This is the next logical move in the long chess match Patriots offensive coordinator Josh McDaniels is playing with the Seattle defense. Since the Seahawks have shown an unwillingness to remove any linebackers from the box as an adjustment to motion, not even bringing them slightly to the edge, that means you can hide a guy like Amendola, stacking him behind another receiver in a short split from the offensive tackle, and the linebacker won't necessarily be involved. This means that there is even more space on the outside of the screen if the defense clogs up the middle, which is what happens.

Amendola approaches this play similar to the way a good tailback approaches the inside zone play. Initially he's going to hit the alley very aggressively. If there is an opening, he should take it. However he should also be mindful of Thomas, the FS, coming into the picture inside the alley, and press the hole between the hash and the numbers with the intention of bringing Thomas closer to the blockers so that he'll get himself blocked, leaving no one else on the outside between Amendola and the end zone once he cuts out.

The pulling guard also helps hold the will linebacker and create the initial point of attack, giving the rest of the offensive line time to do their job and get out into the alley to plow the road and create a path for Amendola.

New England Drive 3 / Play 2 / 1st & 10 / +48 Yard Line / Left Hash / 13:47 2Q

NE – 0 SEA – 0

Summary

Pass incomplete intended for Brandon LaFell to the left side.

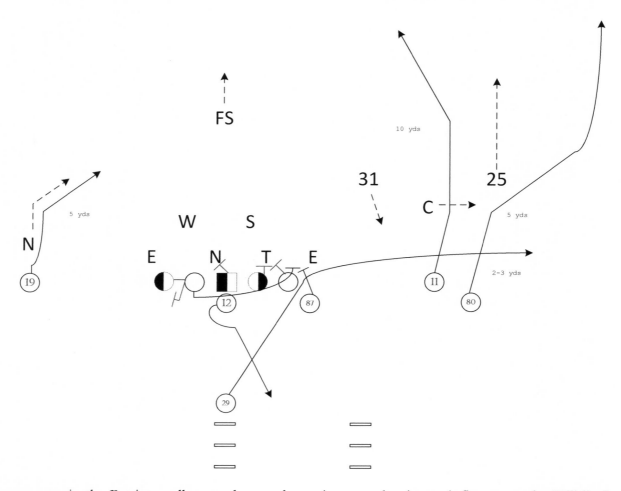

Now once again the Patriots pull a guard on a play action pass, hoping to influence to the Will linebacker, holding him in place so that they can clear out the space behind him to get the football just inside the numbers. Brady mis-times the throw, and when he does get rid of the ball, it's not in a great position and LaFell has to slow down just enough and gives the defender time to recover.

In reality Brady, could've probably reset and found an open receiver to the other side of the field, especially since the FS is aligned just outside the hash, playing a little shallow.

It's an interesting route concept to the 2 receiver bunch side, as well as how Sherman plays the vertical routes. The play is designed to take advantage of Sherman's tendency to play aggressively against the #2 vertical.

New England Drive 3 / Play 3 / 2nd & 10 / +48 Yard Line / Left Hash / 13:25 2Q

NE – 0 SEA – 0

Summary

Pass complete to Brandon LaFell on the hitch route to the left side for a gain of 7 yards.

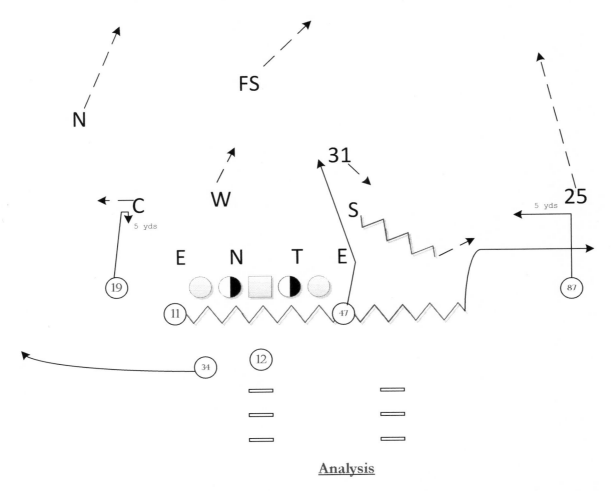

Analysis

Brady eyes the Will linebacker lined up across from the back, and when the Will drops the opposite direction, Brady knows he's got a 2-on-1 situation with Maxwell the corner to the left side, and as soon as LaFell opens up at 5 yards boxing out the corner it's an easy throw for Brady.

His first read in the progression to that side is LaFell on the short hitch route since he's trying to catch up and go from 2nd and long and get to 3rd and medium or better.

If the secondary to the 3 receiver side doesn't adjust to the motion, then Brady is looking to that side first, but as it stands, Seattle is less worried about staying gap sound on 2nd and long, and more worried about getting enough bodies to defend the pass game.

New England Drive 3 / Play 4 / 3rd & 3 / +41 Yard Line / Left Hash / 13:10 2Q

NE – 0 SEA – 0

Summary

Completion to Vereen out of the backfield to the right for a gain of 5 yards and a first down.

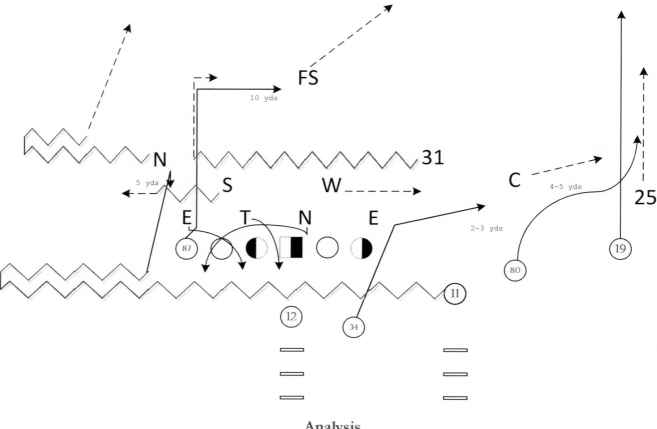

Analysis

As the offense comes to the line, Brady points out the Sam linebacker and slides the protection that way. He releases the running back Vereen on the flat route to the opposite side.

It's all about leverage on the defender as well as the down and distance. It's 3rd and short, and by moving Edelman from right to left, he gets Chancellor to move with him as well, which opens up opportunities for Vereen to that side, since the other 2 routes are designed to clear out the area on the right and create space for the flat route by Vereen. When running the flat route, he manages to find a spot just past the sticks between the two underneath defenders to that side.

Brady didn't try to force anything on this play, he just waited for the guys to do their jobs and let the numbers game play out like it should.

New England Drive 3 / Play 4 / 3rd & 3 / +41 Yard Line / Left Hash / 13:10 2Q

NE – 0 SEA – 0

Summary

Pass incomplete intended for Gronkowski in the deep right side of the field.

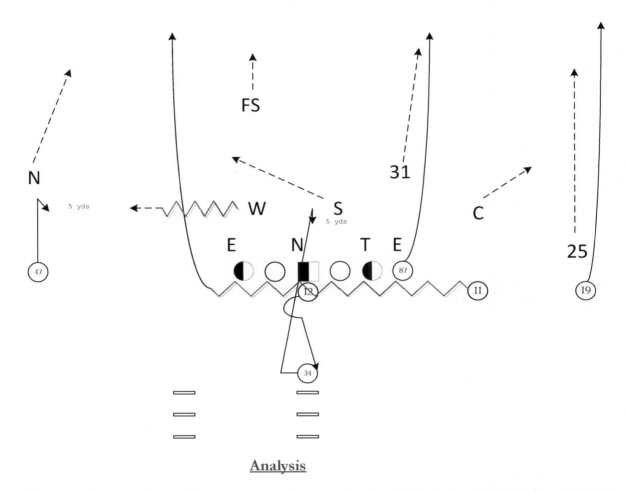

Analysis

The corner Maxwell doesn't chase Edelman in motion across the formation, which forces the Will linebacker to bump over out of the box. To the far left side, the TE Hoomanawanui is split out about 3 yards away from the sideline, and takes the nickel defensive back with him away from the rest of the pass defense scheme.

At the snap, Brady opens up on the play action fake and then sets up in the backfield looking for the FS. Since #29 Thomas is heading toward the seam route by Edelman, so Gronkowski ends up getting the football thrown his way.

Seattle actually plays the same coverage to this formation as they did against the 12 personnel formation to start the game, when both tight ends were split out, one to each side. This was a question of leverage by Sherman to see what he would do with a receiver split across from him instead of a tight end.

Since Sherman is pressing LaFell but the defense is still trying to outnumber the offense 3 to 2 to that side, that means Sherman is not able to get deep quick enough to take away the outside of the vertical route by Gronk, so the only defender really playing the route is Kam Chancellor, playing more over the top than anything else, so Brady puts the ball inside and a little behind but unfortunately for New England Gronk doesn't do a good job adjusting to the pass and can't come back to the ball before it falls incomplete.

If Sherman had played off of LaFell pre-snap, Brady knows there's a real good chance he's going to try to cheat on the #2 vertical and take away Gronk, so it's most likely that Brady just fires it out to the tight end on the field to the left who has a nice cushion over him.

Seattle does a nice job of playing a two-safety coverage out of a 1-high look pre-snap, but it almost costs them.

New England Drive 3 / Play 6 / 2nd & 10 / +36 Yard Line / Right Hash / 11:59 2Q

NE – 0 SEA – 0

Summary

No gain by Vereen up the middle

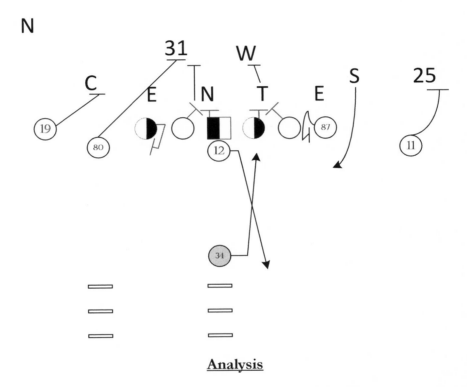

Analysis

Here's another example of the Patriot offense trying to get back on schedule after an incompletion on 1st down.

The Patriots move to 11 personnel with Vereen as the lone back, but decides to get under center and hands it off up the middle in a typical inside zone play where the offensive line fires off the ball.

The DE over the left tackle slants inside the B gap into the backfield, and the Sam linebacker shoots off the edge. Between the two of them, they make contact with Vereen in the backfield stopping him short for no gain.

New England Drive 3 / Play 7 / 3rd & 10 / +36 Yard Line / Right Hash / 11:46 2Q

NE – 0 SEA – 0

Summary

Completion to Edelman over the middle for a gain of 24 yards and a 1st down.

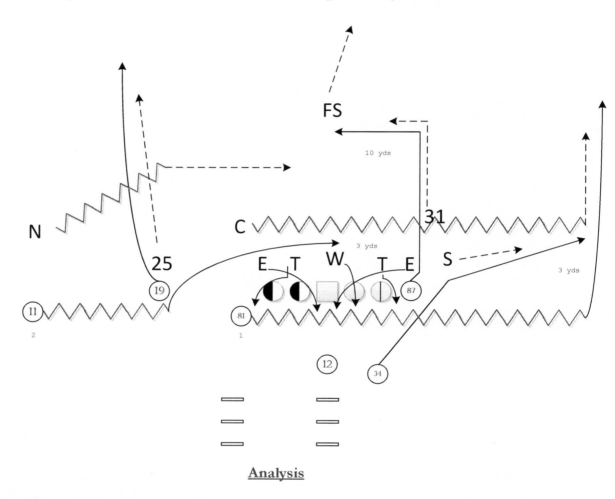

Analysis

Tim Wright #81 comes into the game as the 2nd TE and he's matched up on Maxwell. He goes in motion from left to right taking Maxwell with him.

After surveying the defense now that Wright ends up in his final spot, Brady brings the next man in motion, and once again it's Edelman.

The look from the Patriots is a familiar one, putting the TEs to one side of the formation, and both receivers to the other side in order to force the defense to declare their intentions and to maximize any matchup advantages the offense may have should Seattle decide to go with a more balanced alignment with the guys in the secondary.

The stacked receiver alignment forces #27 the nickel Tharold Simon will have to give ground and line up 3-4 yards deep behind Sherman in the stacked alignment. This creates the space to run the shallow crossing route over the middle.

This read and throw also has a lot to do with leverage and numbers to the TE side. Brady is wary of the alignment to Vereen's side of the formation. Since both the Sam linebacker and Chancellor are aligned far outside against the flat route, so he knows the middle is going to be wide open with the aggressive stance the defensive front is taking. Brady delivers the ball and Edelman breaks a tackle for a long gain on 3rd and long to pick up the 1st down.

The Patriots are most likely thinking that this is 4-down territory, which makes Brady more comfortable with throwing the underneath route and letting Edelman do what he does best. From the current line of scrimmage, it's a 53-yard field goal, and it's a little too close to punt, so if the Patriots can pick up a few yards, they may be able to set up a more manageable 4th down situation.

New England Drive 3 / Play 8 / 1ˢᵗ & 10 / +12 Yard Line / 10:59 2Q

NE – 0 SEA – 0

Summary

Gain of 1 on the run up the middle by Blount

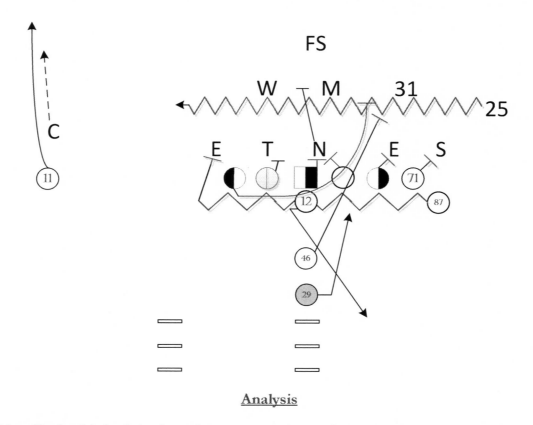

Analysis

Now that New England is back in the red zone on 1st down, they want to test the waters once again with the big guys. The Patriots bring in an extra offensive lineman #71 Cameron Fleming as the 2nd TE, lining up on the line of scrimmage.

This is a curious adjustment by the Patriots, since they pull the backside tackle instead of the guard. This has a couple of advantages. For one thing, they run away from the TE motion which breaks tendencies they've established early in the game.

This also means that the guard is not pulling around and creating a large hole on the backside of the play which would leave the offense vulnerable to penetration, and it also means that the backside guard can occupy the head-up 2 technique, freeing up the center to work with the front side guard on a double team block on the nose.

The play is designed to hit up inside the B gap, which may even hit tighter if the combo on the nose is more successful than expected. It also gets a fullback on the SS, James Develin on Kam Chancellor (Big on big).

New England Drive 3 / Play 9 / 2nd & 9 / +11 Yard Line / Right Hash / 10:09 2Q

NE – 0 SEA – 0

Summary

Touchdown! Pass complete to Brandon LaFell on the quick slant to the left side into the end zone.

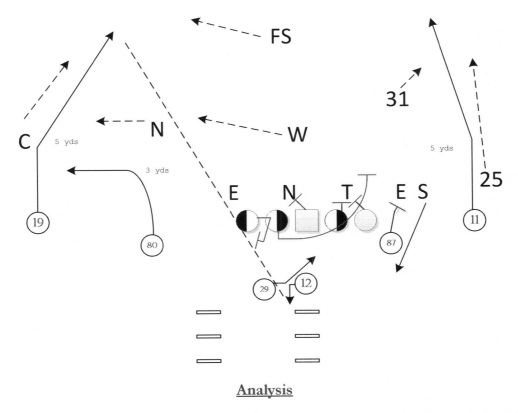

Analysis

New England continues their practice of building off of previous plays in similar situations, and line up to run the same power fake packaged with a slant/flat concept to attack the defenders assigned to the short side.

This time, the nickel completely ignores the play fake by Brady and flies out to cover the flat route by Amendola, which leaves a giants throwing lane open behind him for the slant by LaFell, who catches the TD pass.

This is a perfect example of having answers for each defensive adjustment, even within the confines of the same play. Since the nickel corner obviously anticipated the play coming, he's determined not to repeat his previous mistake of being indecisive. He's decided to cover the flat route completely, and as a result, the window to the end zone emerges for LaFell and Brady.

New England PAT / Seattle PAT Block

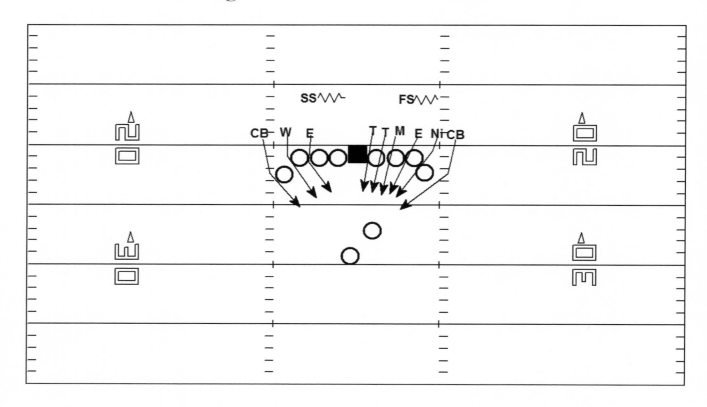

New

New England Drive #3 Review

New England finally punches it in the end zone on this drive after going back to a couple of things they learned from previous drives, and progressing through the game plan to force Seattle to worry about the leverage to the single receiver side.

The first three plays of the drive all focused on attacking the single receiver side of the formation, particularly the area between the left hash and the numbers. In this way, New England offensive coordinator Josh McDaniels can force the linebackers inside the tackle has to be more elastic in their drops, and more willing to vacate the middle of the field.

Notice that New England is not softening up the interior coverage by throwing hitches out wide past the numbers, they are consciously trying to get the inside linebackers moving around and cognizant of that the throw could go right over the top of their heads. It's also no coincidence that the first two plays involved play action fakes that pulled the guard. Once again the Patriots are specifically targeting the inside linebackers in the nickel package, forcing them to be everywhere at once, which undoubtedly will lead to them hesitating and playing worse.

As for the next phase of the game plan, we can already see it come to fruition when New England uses Shane Vereen coming out of the backfield on the flat route to clear out the underneath coverage and open the door for the shallow crossing route by Edelman to pick up the first down.

New England Kickoff

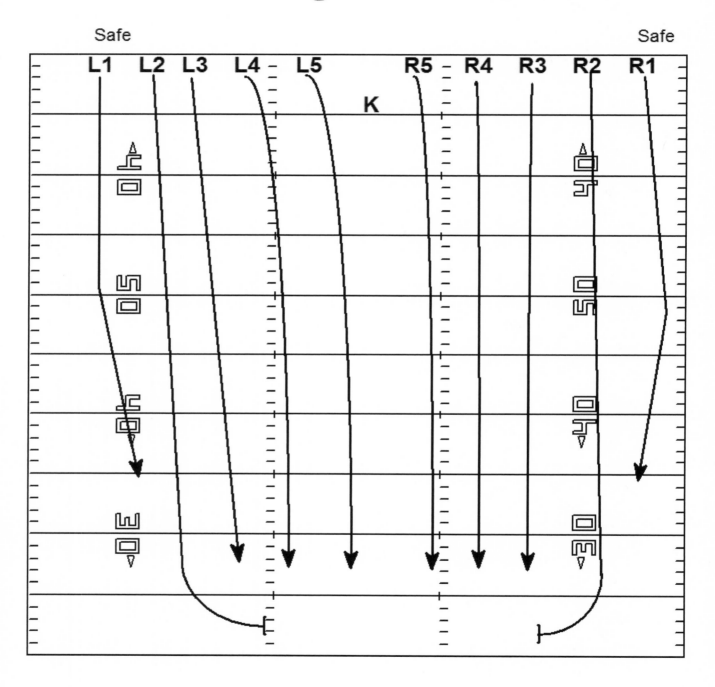

Seattle Kickoff Return

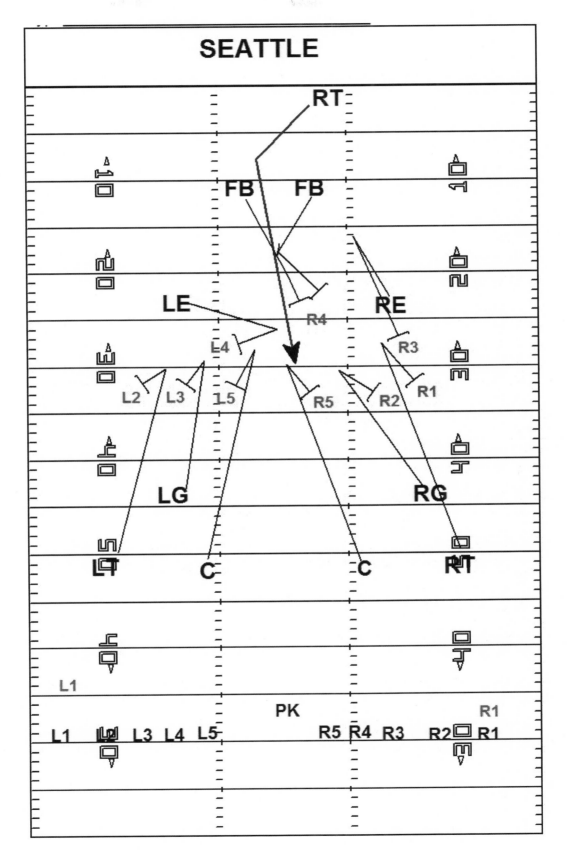

Seattle Drive 3 / Play 1 / 1ˢᵗ & 10 / -20 Yard Line / Middle / 9:47 2Q

NE – 7 SEA – 0

Summary

Sack! Russell Wilson is sacked by Chandler Jones coming off the weak side defensive end position for a loss of 3 yards.

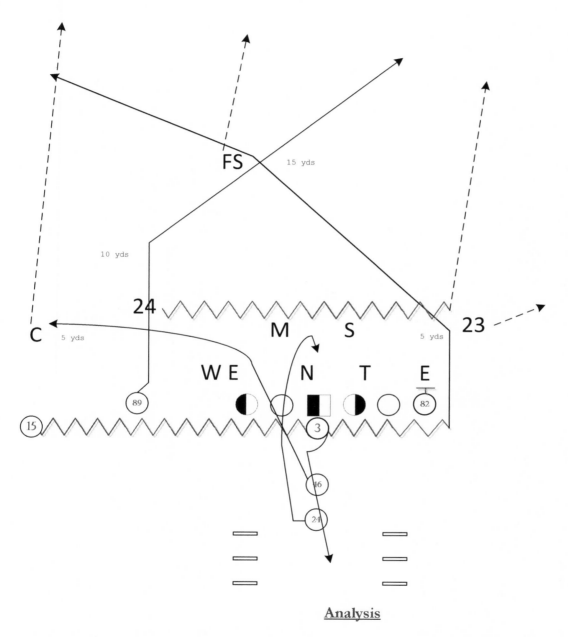

Analysis

Once again Seattle goes for the big play on 1st and 10, but this time the protection breaks down and he's sacked.

After carrying out the play fake, Wilson's eyes go to the deep crossing route by Baldwin, since by following the motion man, Seattle had hoped that Baldwin could rid himself of Revis, but since New England is playing cover 3, Revis ends up covering Baldwin by dropping into the deep 1/3 on his side.

Jones is able to break free on the left side because of conflicting assignments in the pass protection scheme. Since the protection scheme is designed to look like the wide zone scheme that Seattle has run earlier in the game the left tackle has to fire out to the end man on the line of scrimmage, which is the Will backer #55 Akeem Ayers #55.

Jones slants inside the B gap once he sees the tackle fire out, but since the left guard is so occupied with keeping hands on the 1-technique Sealver Siliga that he doesn't get wide enough in time to get a block on Jones, who gets to Wilson just as he turns around after carrying out the play fake and setting his feet.

Seattle Drive 3 / Play 2 / 2nd & 13 / -17 Yard Line / Right Hash / 9:20 2Q

NE – 7 SEA – 0

Summary

Gain of 5 yards by Marshawn Lynch up the middle.

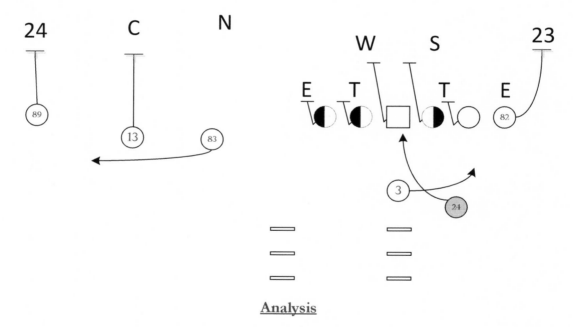

Analysis

Seattle previously ran a zone read play with TE Luke Wilson split out wide to the single receiver side. The structure of the formation is the exact same except that now they've brought in the TE attached to the offensive line, and they want to see if it gives them anything new with Rob Ninkovich. As it happens, Ninkovich puts his hand in the ground in a 3 point stance, and he has to cover the same amount of ground when defending the zone read play.

As expected, Ninkovich plays up the field which signals to Wilson that he needs to hand off the football to Lynch, which he does. Seattle picks up 5 yards and sets up a 3rd and long situation that looks slightly better than it would've otherwise.

Seattle Drive 3 / Play 3 / 3rd & 8 / -22 Yard Line / Right Hash / 8:47 2Q

NE – 7 SEA – 0

Summary

Pass incomplete intended for Jermain Kearse deep down the right sideline.

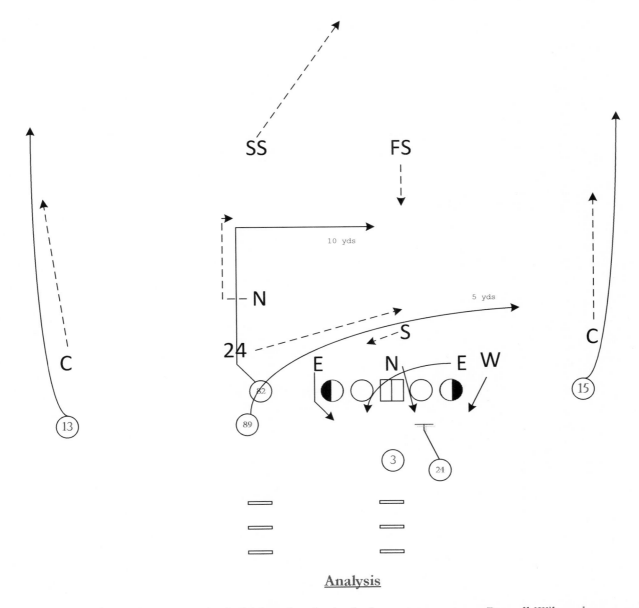

Analysis

The Patriots roll down into a single-high safety look playing man coverage. Russell Wilson keeps one eye on the FS, and once he sees him come downhill at the snap, he knows he's going to go after the long bomb to Jermain Kearse on the fade to the right.

Since New England drops a safety into the middle of the field, Seattle feels as though their best option is to test the one-on-one matchups to the outside. Baldwin is running free underneath on the drive route, but since he's being chased by Revis, Wilson doesn't like his chances of making a play after the catch to pick up the 1st down.

Seattle Punt

PRO PUNT 55 SAFE

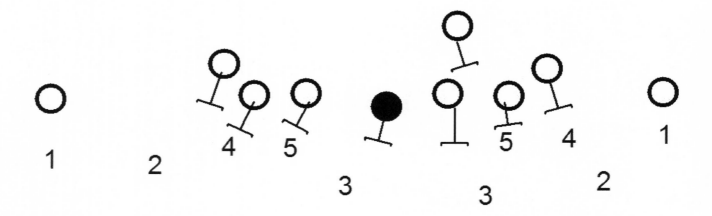

New England Punt Return

55 SAFE   SAFE RET

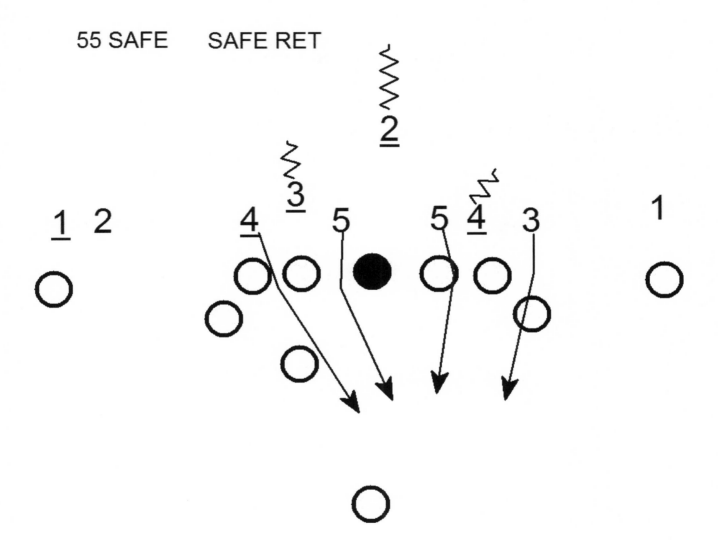

Seattle Drive #3 Review

Seattle gives New England a few more things to think about on this drive. One gets the sense that these are things Darrell Bevell wanted to get out of the way much earlier, but had to wait until the 3rd drive midway through the 2nd quarter because his offense has 1 first down and 0 completions, meaning that they cannot extend drives and give Bevel more chances to test the defense with different looks.

On 1st down the offense lines up in "21" personnel (or "regular" personnel depending on your terminology) for the first time in the game, and New England brings on their 4-3 personnel in response. They align the "overhang" LB to the twins side, because the SS would be matched up in pass coverage on the TE anyway, so the Patriots don't need two edge guys aligned to the same side of the formation. The Patriots show a 3-deep zone on 1st down after the Seattle sends Kearse in motion from left to right.

The next new look they give the defense is the shotgun with a back offset to the same side as the TE, which creates an extra gap for the defense to be concerned with, and at the same time, Bevel is continuing to test the option responsibilities of the players in the defensive front by giving them different looks and seeing how they react.

Nothing changes for Rob Ninkovich when it comes to how he plays against the back to his side. When running the zone play away from the tight end and leaving the strong side DE unblocked, it may slow up the pursuit and force Ninkovich to widen in this instance, but the assignment doesn't change much.

New England Drive 4 / Play 1 / 1ˢᵗ & 10 / -28 Yard Line / Right Hash / 8:05 2Q

NE – 7 SEA – 0

Summary

Pass incomplete, knocked down at the line of scrimmage by the defensive tackle #99 Tony McDaniel.

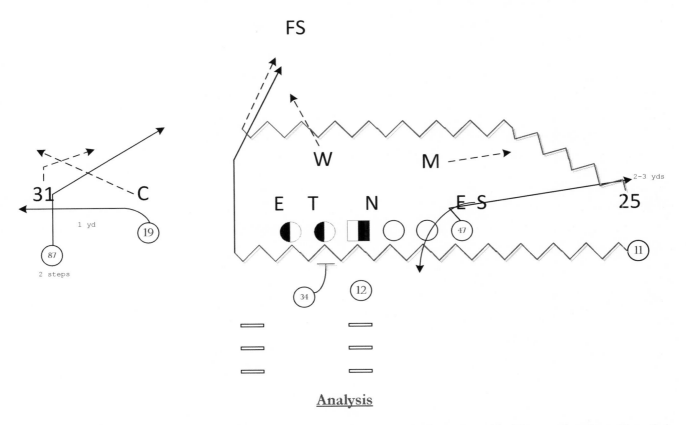

Analysis

The Patriots bring Edelman in motion from right to left, taking Sherman with him to the slot side of the formation.

They've also got Gronk split out wide to the left, forcing Chancellor to take him.

The slant route by Edelman occupies the Will linebacker's drop, opening up the route on the outside by Gronk, which is where Brady is trying to go with the football. Unfortunately for New England, the pass is knocked down at the line. If it's not tipped away, the pass is most likely completed for a first down (at a minimum).

The first play the New England offense gets back on the field, they go right after Jeremy Lane's replacement Tharold Simon by creating a natural rub between Gronk and LaFell.

New England Drive 4 / Play 2 / 2ⁿᵈ & 10 / -28 Yard Line / Right Hash / 8:01 2Q

NE – 7 SEA – 0

Summary

Pass complete underneath to Edelman for a gain of 7 yards.

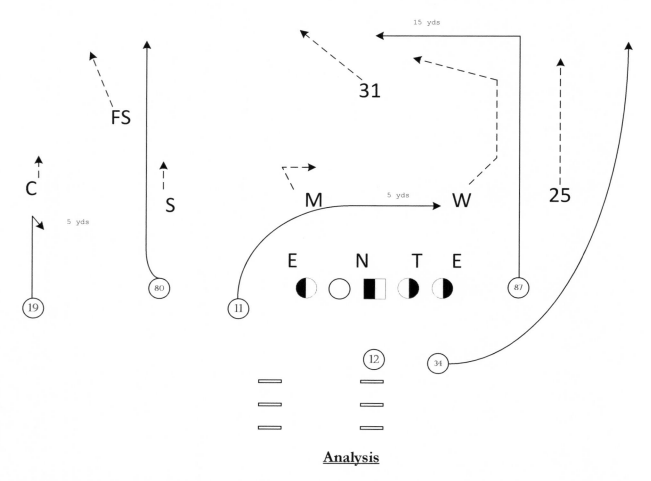

Analysis

The Patriots go back to the basics on 2nd and long, with a play designed to create a "triangle" to the right side of the field. With all three receivers to this side running routes that hit outside of the right hash, Brady's read is a pretty easy one. Depending on the structure of the defense, it could turn into more of an "area" read, but in this particular situation Brady is eyeing the Will linebacker and throwing away from him.

As soon as he sees the Will drop with Gronkowski's vertical release, he knows the window is going to be clean for Edelman.

He picks up 7 yards on the catch but Bobby Wagner runs him down and makes the tackle from behind and stops him from picking up the 1st down.

Drive 4 / Play 3 / 3rd & 3 / -35 Yard Line / Right Hash / 7:41 2Q

NE – 7 SEA – 0

Summary

Pass incomplete, intended for Edelman

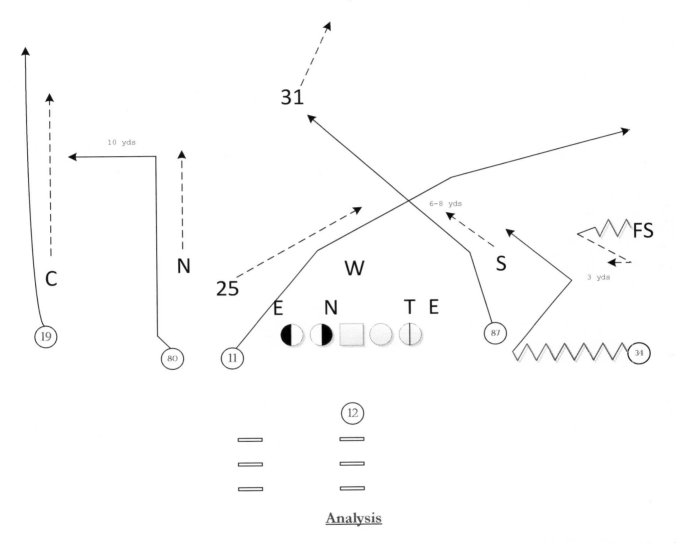

Analysis

The Patriots line up in empty and find another way to use Gronkowski's size without making him the primary receiver.

This is designed as a "rule" (or pick) play to get Edelman open days to the right side of the field. Based on the pre-snap alignment, this is going to be man coverage, so Brady will be looking to the middle-to-right side of the field, whereas if it was more of a zone look, this left side of the play would look a lot more attractive, since the 10-yard out route will be open as the slot receiver replaces the corner dropping to the deep 1/3 to his side.

Edelman ends up getting tripped up as he tries to get past the mesh point with Gronkowski, and the pass is incomplete.

New England Punt

PRO PUNT55 BASE

2   3   4   5   5   4   3   2   1

1

Seattle Punt Return

55 BASE   8 MAN BLOCK

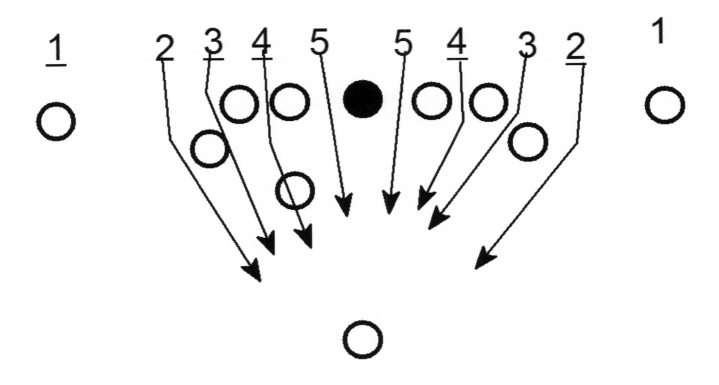

New England Drive #3

The Patriots manages to create open receivers on all three plays in the series, but Brady wasn't able to get a clean pocket on two of them. Credit the Seattle defense for being physical at the line of scrimmage and down the field in coverage. The physical play of the defense is what leads to this 3 and out, because on paper this looked like 3 consecutive first downs.

At the very least, New England still manages to get Edelman open on a shallow crossing route again for a 7 yard gain. Josh McDaniels calls the same play that got #47 Michael Hoomanawanui the ball on the hitch route two drives earlier, but this time the ball goes to the shallow route.

The Seahawks have been playing zone almost exclusively to these 3x1 sets from New England, so by bringing the shallow route from the other side New England is hoping to hit an area vacated by the underneath defenders who have chased the vertical routes by Vereen and Gronk to this side, but Seattle's linebackers have been coached up that in this matchup zone coverage, if you see #3 coming across on a shallow crossing route you should be playing him man-to-man so that the defense has bodies to that side in case the route is thrown.

It's Wagner's tackle of Edelman on the shallow route that helps keep this to a 3 and out.

Seattle Drive 4 / Play 1 / 1st & 10 / -30 Yard Line / Left Hash / 7:07 2Q

NE – 7 SEA – 0

Summary

Gain of 5 yards by Marshawn Lynch on the carry up the middle.

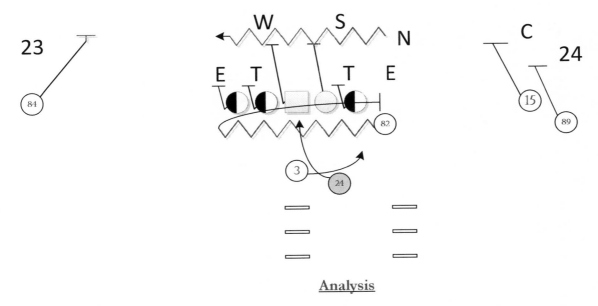

Analysis

By moving the TE Wilson in motion to the opposite side of the formation and then bringing him back across, Seattle hopes to gain a man to the "wham" side since the nickel corner will probably get lost in the mess to the left side of the play and get himself blocked by coming downhill too quickly and losing track of where the TE is going.

This is a play that usually hits to the "wham" side even though Lynch initially heads away from the movement of the TE. The idea is that the offensive line will create enough movement on the defensive front to get them to move to the left, and since the backside defensive end will fly up the field, there will be an extra gap to the right side. Once again, this is where a guy like Vince Wilfork comes in. Initially, he's double-teamed by the right tackle and guard, but eventually the guard has to come off of the block once he sees the Sam linebacker coming down to make a play on the run, which leaves the tackle one-on-one with Wilfork. It's a battle he can't win, and in fact all three defenders to that side of the play shed their blocks and help bring down Lynch.

Seattle Drive 4 / Play 2 / 2ⁿᵈ & 5 / -35 Yard Line / Right Hash / 6:42 2Q

NE – 7 SEA – 0

Summary

Gain of 4 yards by Marshawn Lynch up the middle.

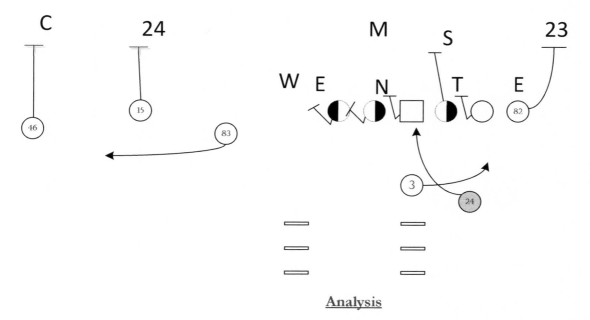

Analysis

With "regular" (21) personnel back in the game for the Seattle offense, New England sends their base personnel group on the field as well. The Patriots line up their Will linebacker Akeem Ayers just a bit wider than the defensive end to that side, and he's keeping his eyes on Wilson. Because Lynch is aligned away from the uncovered receiver in the slot, Lockette, Wilson would have to raise up and just throw the ball instead of having the ability to fake it to Lynch first to time up the throw, in other words, if it's a pass to the uncovered receiver, Wilson will open up to his left, and if it's a run, Wilson will open up to his right. As a result, Ayers can afford to be a little more aggressive in his alignment. If on the other hand, Lynch was aligned to the 3 receiver side, then Ayers would have to honor the threat of the uncovered guy by at least splitting the difference between the receiver and the offensive tackle. Still, if Wilson wanted to, he could take a shot at the bubble route, but since Seattle is right where they want to be on 2nd and medium, the offense is content to play conservative and hand it off.

The Patriots actually outnumber the Seahawks in the tackle box, but thanks to some decisive running by Marshawn Lynch, combined with his ability to fall forward, Seattle sets up 3rd and short. The offensive line is able to create just enough movement that a crease appears for Lynch for a split second and he takes advantage of it.

Seattle Drive 4 / Play 2 / 2ⁿᵈ & 5 / -35 Yard Line / Right Hash / 6:42 2Q

NE – 7 SEA – 0

Summary

No play, false start penalty

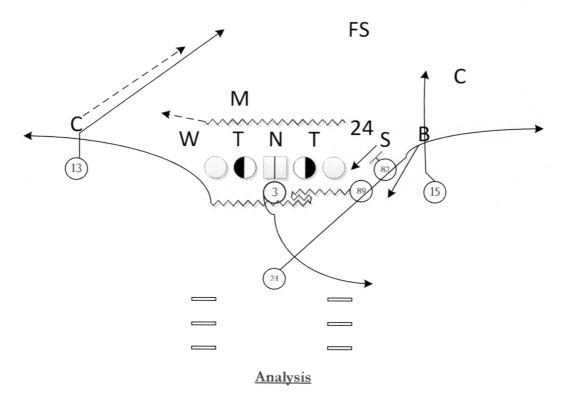

Analysis

Before the play has time to really develop, it appears that Seattle is trying to run a variation of the backside wheel concept that they called earlier in the game, only this time it's likely that the front side of the play is the intended target, since they're sending Doug Baldwin in motion, meaning that Revis is going with him.

By taking the Patriots' best cover man away from the bunch side, Seattle is trying to create some opportunities toward the strong side for the corner-flat combination.

Unfortunately for Seattle, a false start penalty whistles the play dead before anything can happen.

Seattle Drive 4 / Play 4 / 3rd & 6 / -34 Yard Line / Middle / 5:50 2Q

NE – 7 SEA – 0

Summary

Pass complete to Jermaine Kearse running the hitch route on the right side for a gain of 6 yards and the first down.

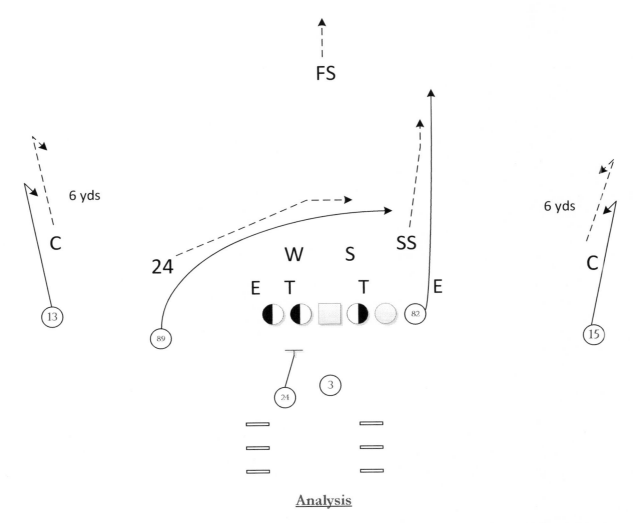

Analysis

Because of the alignment of the defense, Wilson knows there's a pretty good chance that McCourty at the SS position will carry the vertical route by Wilson, and if he doesn't, that means there's probably going to a window in the zone coverage from about 7-10 yards once McCourty widens to the flat or blitzes. As a result, this means that Kearse #15 on the outside will likely be one-on-one running a route that's just long enough to pick up the first down. This play is designed to attack the right side, so if neither of those two routes are open, then you've got a crossing route coming in late behind the vertical route by the TE Wilson.

Once Wilson takes the snap, his instincts are confirmed and he fires a bullet to Kearse out to the right side and just barely picks up the 1st down.

Seattle Drive 4 / Play 5 / 1ˢᵗ & 10 / -40 Yard Line / Right Hash / 5:05 2Q

NE – 7 SEA – 0

Summary

Gain of 5 yards from Marshawn Lynch on the carry up the middle.

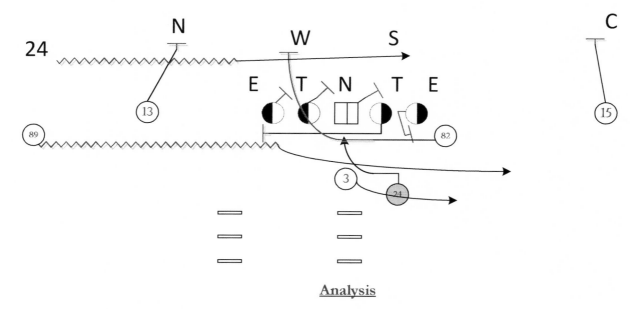

Analysis

Nothing really advanced about this play, it's just the old-school counter concept with a jet sweep fake thrown in for good measure.

New England has their heavy package on the field right now with three defensive tackles aligned over the center and both guards. The message is clear, the Patriots are putting some muscle into stopping the run, but for the first time today, the Seahawks come at them with a gap scheme instead of a zone scheme.

The jet sweep fake causes just enough hesitation in the defensive front so that the pullers can get a head start on the defense, and even though the Sam and Will fill their gaps correctly, Lynch manages to pick up five yards.

Seattle Drive 4 / Play 6 / 2ⁿᵈ & 5 / -45 Yard Line / Left Hash / 4:35 2Q

NE – 7 SEA – 0

Summary

Pass complete to Chris Matthews down the right sideline for a gain of 44 yards.

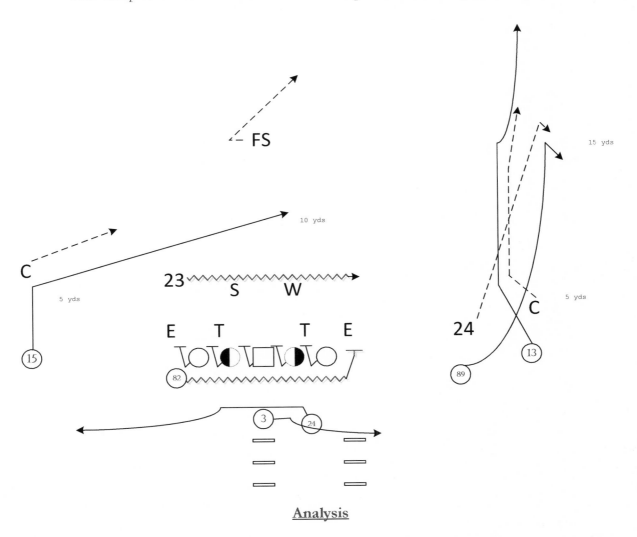

Analysis

The movement of Luke Wilson from left to right accomplishes a couple of things: It opens the passing window on the backside (most of the time at least, since on this particular play the linebackers do a good job of not biting on the play fake), and it also means that the front side edge is protected for the boot play.

As for the front side pass concept where the receivers cross up, it's a small wrinkle on a pass pattern that Seattle has run a couple of times in 2014. Normally, the outside receiver, #13 Chris Matthews in this case, would break inside on a curl route at the same time Doug Baldwin breaks out on the comeback. It also helps that by design of the play Seattle keeps the Patriots' best cover guy Revis underneath the deeper route and takes him out of the play so he can't be a factor down the field.

Matthews makes an incredible catch that puts the Seahawks in great position to tie the game.

Seattle Drive 4 / Play 7 / 1ˢᵗ & 10 / +11 Yard Line / Right Hash / 4:05 2q

NE – 7 SEA – 0

Summary

Gain of 4 yards by Marshawn Lynch on the carry up the middle.

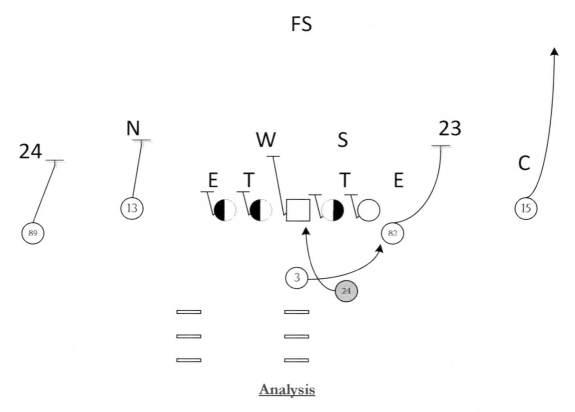

Analysis

Once again, Wilson hands it off to Lynch on the zone read play to Lynch up the middle, with the Will linebacker Collins and the unblocked DE Ninkovich making the tackle 4 yards down the field, setting up another 2nd and medium. This is a play where Seattle hurries up to the line in order to catch New England off guard or especially Ninkovich playing sloppy technique when he's in a hurry.

Worst-case scenario, you hand it off to Lynch for a couple of yards, but if they can catch Ninkovich sticking his nose a little too far inside, Wilson can take off around the corner with the TE blocking out in the alley on Patrick Chung.

Hightower does a good job of recognizing the combo developing right in front of him, and crashing into the A gap. As a result, he pushes the play further outside to Ninkovich, and because Hightower occupies the combo block at the line of scrimmage instead of 3-4 yards down the field, it's a lot easier for Collins to come from the backside and help on the tackle.

Seattle Drive 4 / Play 8 / 2nd & 6 / +7 Yard Line / Right Hash / 3:17 2Q

NE – 7 SEA – 0

Summary

Gain of 4 yards on the carry by Marshawn Lynch along the left side.

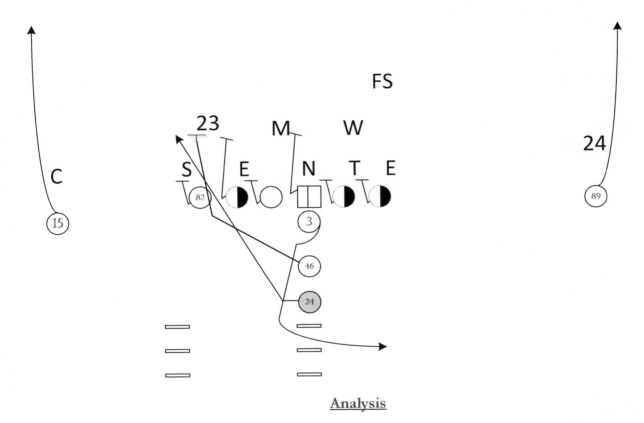

Analysis

The defensive end Chandler Jones fires off the line and comes across so quickly that he forces the left guard back on his heels, and the force of the collision knocks the helmet off the guard's head. As Jones is able to shed the block he gets his hands on Lynch and brings him down after a gain of four yards.

The play is designed to hit in the C gap, and if Chandler Jones doesn't come off the line the way he does and defeat the blocker in front of him, Lynch strolls into the end zone practically untouched.

The safeties are balanced pre-snap, with one to either side, which makes it easier for Wilson to confirm that the play is being called in the right direction, since Seattle has a numbers advantage to the left side, and then there's the fact that they're running away from Wilfork.

Seattle Drive 4 / Play 9 / 3rd & 2 / + 3 Yard Line / Left Hash / 2:36 2Q

NE – 7 SEA – 0

Summary

Touchdown! Marshawn Lynch carries the ball to the right for a 3 yard gain and a score.

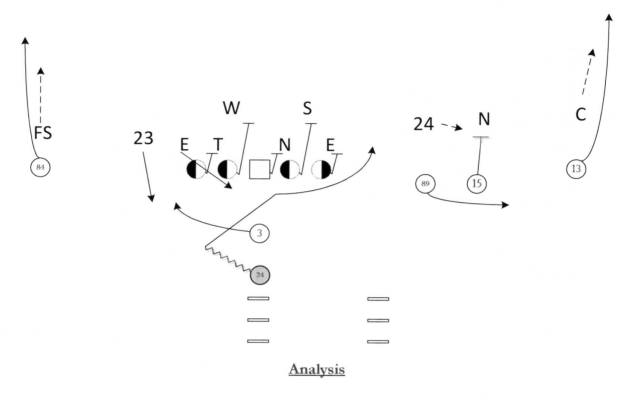

Analysis

The bubble route in the slot by Baldwin opens up the alley for Lynch when the play is bounced outside. Revis is locked up in man coverage over the top of Baldwin, so he's gonna go wherever his man goes.

You see Patrick Chung come off the edge at an angle that will allow him to play the QB on the keeper if Wilson decides to try to keep the ball around the left side on the zone read. Then there is the defensive end Chandler Jones who is closing tight down the line of scrimmage in pursuit of Lynch on the give.

This is a wide zone play, which explains why Russell Wilson checked it to the three receiver side, with all that pressure coming from the left. The right tackle engages Ninkovich and manages to get him parallel before turning him inside. The right alley opens up and Lynch crosses the goal line for the score.

This is a great example of offensive coordinator Darrell Bevel using formations and personnel groups to his advantage. With the TE #84 Cooper Helfet in the game and split out to the left as the single receiver to that side, Bevel is hoping to catch the defense bringing a disproportionate amount of pressure from that side, or at least putting their numbers to that side, since the TE strength is to the left but the Seahawks have numbers to the right. That's exactly what happens, and Seattle uses strategy and fundamentals to open up a running lane on the goal line.

Seattle PAT / New England PAT Block

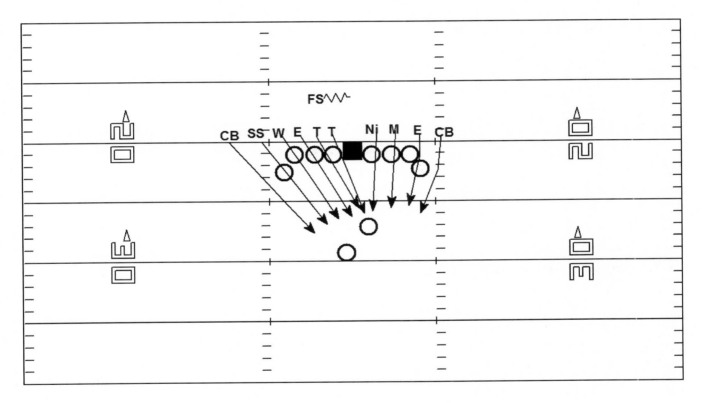

Seattle Drive #4 Review

Seattle has finally found something that works for them in the run game, namely taking the TE off the line of scrimmage and involving him in multiple ways in the blocking schemes up front.

The Seahawks used TE Luke Wilson to motion across the formation and change the run strength to create numbers to one side or the other, pulling him across on a "wham" block on the opposite DE, pulling him across to cut up inside the kickout blocker and pull up into the gap to get a body on the inside linebacker on a counter play, protecting the edge on a boot play, and "arc" releasing on another zone play to influence the DE to that side.

Using the TE in so many ways by putting him off the line of scrimmage means that Seattle has the ability to call the kind of run schemes that you'd normally have to put in new personnel on the field to do. As a result, that three-receiver personnel package that looked like it had a limited run game now has opened the playbook on the defense, and there are now so many different things the Patriots have to worry about.

It's obvious that Bill Belichick was concerned about stopping the run, since on the 7th play of the drive, he actually brings in an extra defensive tackle to play head up over the center. The defense actually got two bodies on Lynch right at the line of scrimmage, but as we discussed during the 1st drive breakdown, 2 is the minimum number of people you need to be able to bring down Lynch. He brings so much force with him that he wills his way to a 5-yard gain.

The adjustments in Seattle's pass game are also evident, since they have moved to attacking the wide areas of the field, finding ways to isolate their receivers and giving them an opportunity to make the play.

With both the hitch play on 3rd and 6, and the long bomb to Chris Matthews 2 plays later, Belichick forced Wilson to make the deep and outside throws, and he did (though not without a lot of help from Matthews on the big pass and catch down the field).

Darrell Bevell used information from earlier in the game to help him make the play call down at the 3 yard line for the score.

After lining up with the TE all alone to the single receiver side on the first drive of the game, Bevell takes note of the fact that the Patriots set their strength to that side, and brings out the formation again, hoping to get the exact look he gets on this play. New England puts extra bodies to the single receiver side, which opens the potential to the pass strength for an open running lane in the alley.

It should also be noted that Belichick has stuck almost exclusively to "balanced" looks on defense, with both defensive tackles aligned in 3 techniques, both defensive ends lined up off the shoulder of the offensive tackles in a five technique, and two inside linebackers in the box, the base alignment of the 4-2 nickel package the Patriots have been playing much of the game. Even when they bring on an extra defensive tackle, they'll align head up on the center while most of the defensive front plays their same responsibilities. In other words, for most of the drive, until the final play, the defense is keeping equal numbers up front to both sides of the formation.

Even when Seattle moves the tight end from one side of the formation to the other the numbers stay the same up front since the strong safety usually is matched up with him and runs with him in motion. In this way, through the use of balanced defensive fronts and man coverage on the tight end it becomes next to impossible for Seattle to get a true numbers advantage through motion and shifts to either side of the formation.

 New England's defense is doing a decent job of recognizing the plays as they develop, but the different motions and movement on defense are creating hesitation, not to mention the fact that they have to tackle Marshawn Lynch, which is no easy task on its own.

To go back to the pre-game notes, it's very simple, the Patriots need to do their job on defense, nothing more.

Seattle Kickoff

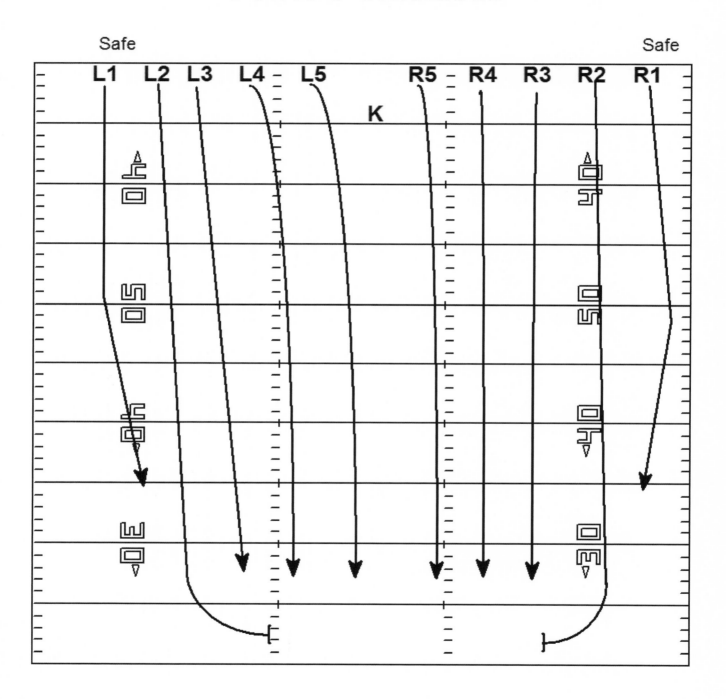

New England Kickoff Return

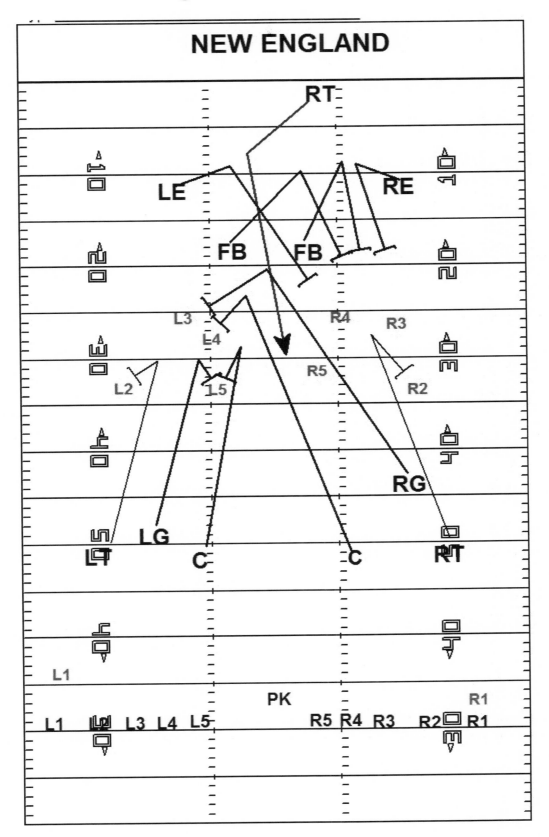

New England Drive 5 / Play 1 / 1ˢᵗ & 10 / -20 Yard Line / Middle / 2:16 2Q

NE – 7 SEA – 7

Summary

Pass complete to Amendola for a gain of 11 yards and a first down

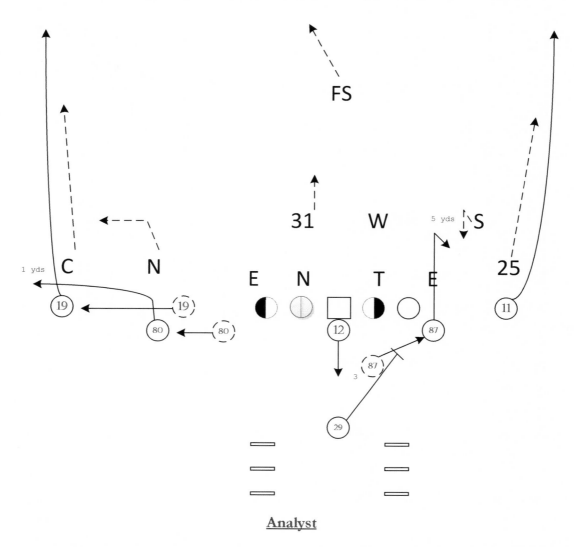

Analyst

Brady widens the receivers out to the left to give them room to run the fade/out concept, and Amendola now has room to cut back inside as he gets away from Maxwell after the catch and picks up the 1st down.

This was very likely a run that was audibled to a quick pass when Brady didn't like what he saw up front. For one thing, the initial tight splits of the receivers signal that the Patriots are trying to get them in position to get blocks on members the secondary on other defenders in the box. Not to mention the fact that Blount is in the backfield, Brady is under center and it's 1st and 10. New England is looking to get ahead of the count of 1st down since they've thrown an incomplete pass the past several 1st and 10s, and have ended up in the hole on 2nd and long.

New England Drive 5 / Play 2 / 1ˢᵗ & 10 / -31 Yard Line / Left Hash / 2:00 2Q

NE – 7 SEA – 7

Summary

Gain of 9 on the run by Blount on the right side.

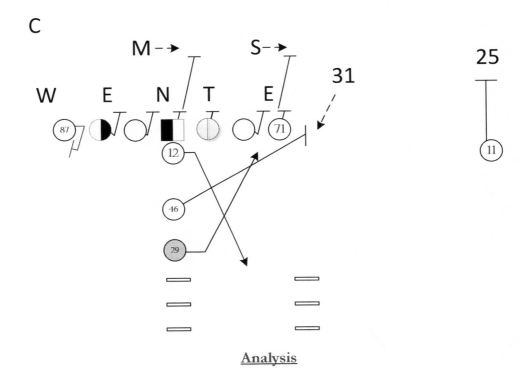

Analysis

The defense switches things up yet again by moving Chancellor up on the line of scrimmage to the #71 side of the formation in order to set the edge and play the kick out block of the fullback. Part of the question Seattle has to answer is how complex New England will get in the short yardage/22 personnel package, and so far they haven't shown much out of the ordinary.

The look is pretty good to the right side, and Brady's call is vindicated when Blount is able to cut off the fullback's block off the butt of the tight end in the D gap, and pick up 9 yards when the Patriots create a good seal in the alley.

Seattle is also starting to recognize that for whatever reason, New England does not want to run toward Gronkowski's side of the formation, most likely because Josh McDaniels believes Fleming is a better blocker on the edge.

New England Drive 5 / Play 3 / 2ⁿᵈ & 1 / -40 Yard Line / Right Hash / 1:40 2Q

NE – 7 SEA – 7

Summary

Pass complete to Vereen out to the right flat for a gain of five yards and a first down.

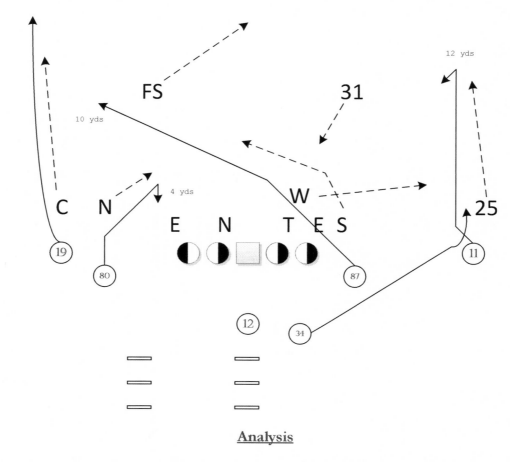

Analysis

Another 3rd down and short where New England decides to throw the ball. Brady pretty much knows where he's going with the pass before the ball is even snapped. Unless the Will backer flies out to the flat with incredible speed, Vereen's free release out of the backfield is enough to give him a head start out on the edge, and all he has to do is pick up one yard, Brady delivers the ball to his inside shoulder and puts it where it's an easy catch.

New England Drive 5 / Play 4 / 1ˢᵗ & 10 / -45 Yard Line / Right Hash / 1:19 2Q

NE – 7 SEA – 7

Summary

Pass incomplete out to Amendola on the deep left side of the field.

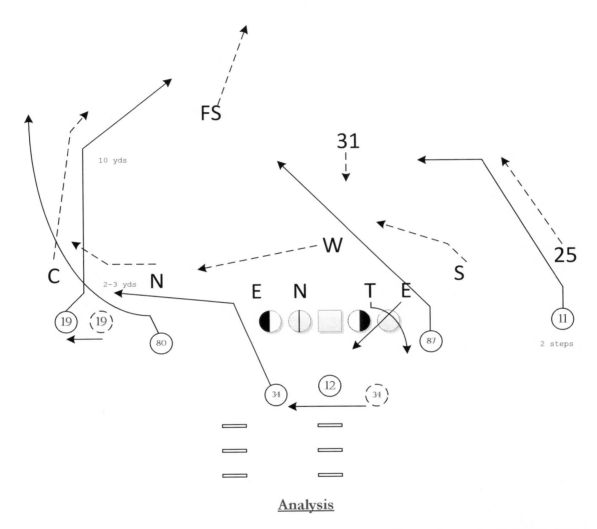

Analysis

On this play, Brady makes another change at the line, moving Vereen over to the left side and widening LaFell out wide to the left at the bottom of the numbers.

At the snap Brady is staring at Earl Thomas looking to see which way he'll drop, since he's looking to get the ball to Edelman down the sideline. By the time the two receivers are crossing each other's paths in the route, Brady is already releasing the ball to a spot down the deep sideline. If the FS Thomas hesitates or makes the read any cloudier, Brady can simply dump it off to Vereen on the flat route.

The pass falls incomplete, since Brady put the ball in an exact spot, and Amendola doesn't quite fade away to the sideline like Brady wants him to, instead staying tight to Maxwell, perhaps expecting the ball a bit deeper.

New England Drive 5 / Play 5 / 2nd & 10 / -45 Yard Line / Right Hash / 0:54 2Q

NE – 7 SEA – 7

Summary

Gain of six yards on the jet sweep to Edelman on the left perimeter.

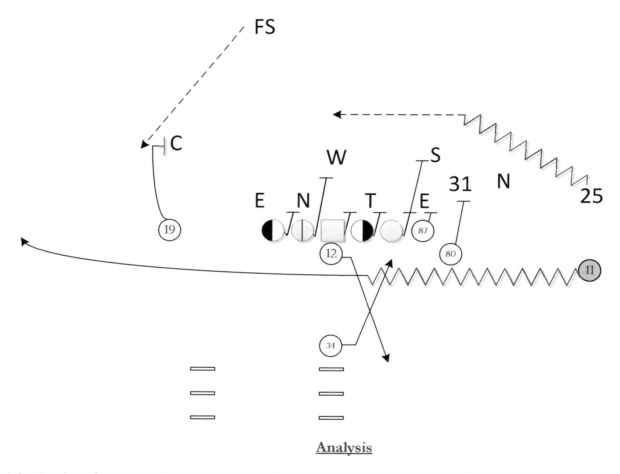

Analysis

The Patriots force Seattle into an uncomfortable alignment, since the 3x1 wing alignment creates an extra gap that the defense has to account for.

New England packages the jet sweep with an outside zone look, which holds the front side of the defense in place, and the tight split of LaFell to the left side of the formation creates a tremendous amount of space to the left side of the formation, and he's got enough of an angle on Earl Thomas the free safety where he nearly blocks the corner and the free safety at the same time.

Edelman avoids the defensive end on the backside of the offensive line, and nearly picks up the 1st down before getting out of bounds and stopping the clock.

New England Drive 5 / Play 6 / 1ˢᵗ & 10 / +43 Yard Line / Left Hash / 0:49 2Q

NE – 7 SEA – 7

Summary

(Previous unlisted play was an offsides call against the defense for a first down)

Pass complete to Vereen underneath for a gain of 16 yards and a first down.

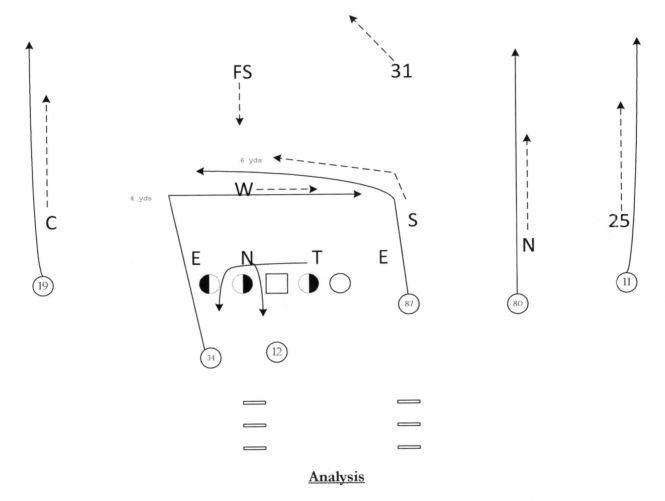

Analysis

The structure of the play is designed to stretch and clear out the defense on the perimeter and create space underneath for Gronk or Vereen depending on who is left open after the mesh point.

Brady delivers the ball and Vereen has it in his hands at the moment Gronk is crossing over the top of him, and once he makes the catch he's got all kinds of green grass in front of him as he picks up the 1st down.

New England Drive 5 / Play 7 / 1ˢᵗ & 10 / +27 Yard Line / Right Hash / 0:40 2Q

NE – 7 SEA – 7

Summary

Pass complete to Vereen in the right flat for a gain of four yards.

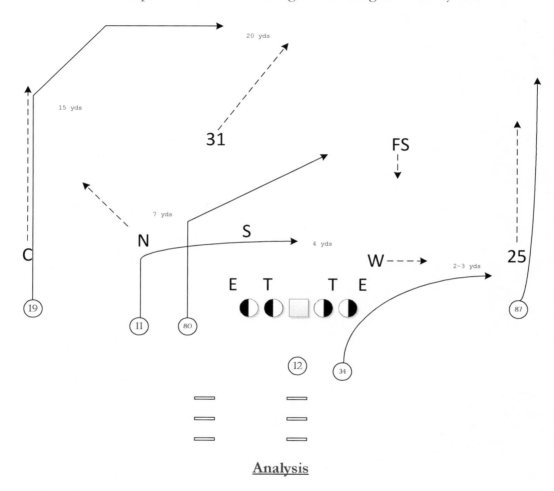

Analysis

Vereen is becoming Brady's go-to receiver in clutch situations, as he takes the quick flat route and gets out of bounds. KJ Wright is locked in tight, but it's a testament to the connection that Brady and Vereen have that he's able to put the ball anywhere near him and he'll come up with the catch.

Also of note is that Gronk is split out wide and Sherman comes with him, carrying the vertical route from Gronk and opening up the flats for Vereen.

New England Drive 5 / Play 8 / 2nd & 6 / +23 Yard Line / Right Hash / 0:36 2Q

NE – 7 SEA – 7

Summary

Touchdown! Pass complete to the deep right side to Gronkowski for a gain of 23 yards and a score.

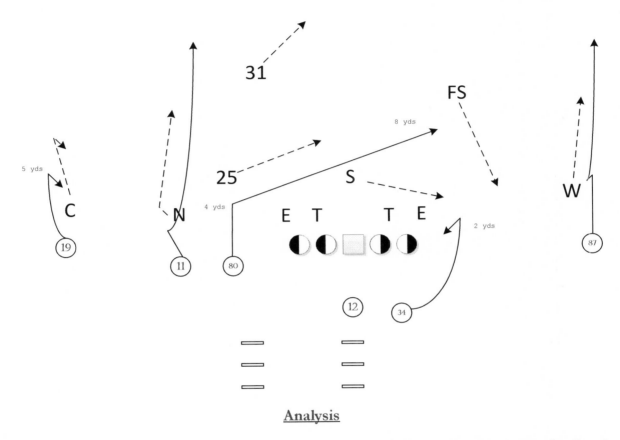

Analysis

New England goes back to another version of a crossing concept with a deep vertical route by Gronkowski designed to clear out space for the crossing routes and the underneath routes.

At the same time, Gronk is matched up against KJ Wright to the single receiver side, and Earl Thomas, who is lined up on the opposite hash, ends up being the middle of the field player once the ball is snapped and the two-deep shell rotates to a single-high look.

Gronk going vertical wasn't an audible, but he wasn't the primary target in the progression until Brady looked over and saw a large mismatch on the outside.

Brady puts the ball where only Gronk can get it, and the Patriots take the lead late in the half.

New England PAT / Seattle PAT Block

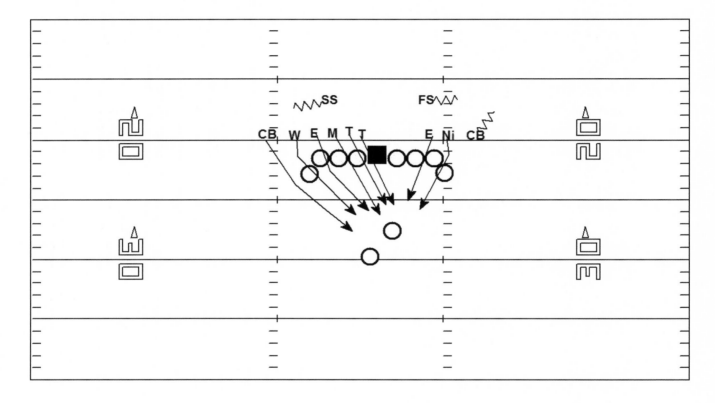

New England Drive #5 Review

The Patriots have already done a lot in this game to exploit the "compressed" side of their formations, whether that's with one receiver lined up tight to the offensive tackle or two receivers aligned close enough to one another to switch routes as they release down the field. This is something that Dan Quinn is going to have to go over with his team at the half, because it's a major part of the game plan for New England up to his point.

From the first play of the drive, when New England starts in that compressed look and then shifts the receivers out wider, to the jet sweep with Edelman (which if not for a tremendous play by Earl Thomas out on the edge would've gone for much longer), much of the drive focused on making sure that the defense to the edge is always wrong.

Seattle put a lot of effort into inserting Kam Chancellor into the middle of the formation in their latest adjustment to take away the shallow crossing route, and it's actually their attempts to disguise their coverage that opens the door to Shane Vereen's big catch and run on Play 6.

It has a lot to do with the kind of coverage that Seattle has been showing to this formation, since up to this point it's been almost entirely Seattle's version of their cover 4/6 matchup zone that makes sure they outnumber the offensive receivers in pass coverage to both sides of the formation. They give a 2-deep look pre-snap, but once the ball is snapped, Kam attempts to rotate down into the middle of the field the way he's been doing for the whole drive so far.

However, when trying to rotate into the middle of the field his path is blocked by Gronkowski as he comes across the field. So now the passing window is wide open for Vereen and he picks up 16 yards and the 1st down. Then on the final scoring play, it's the 1st time Seattle has put a linebacker out lined up over the top of Gronkowski, and Brady takes advantage of it.

So far Seattle has come out with adjustments to everything the Patriots have thrown at them, and New England has responded with a new wrinkle of their own.

New England Kickoff

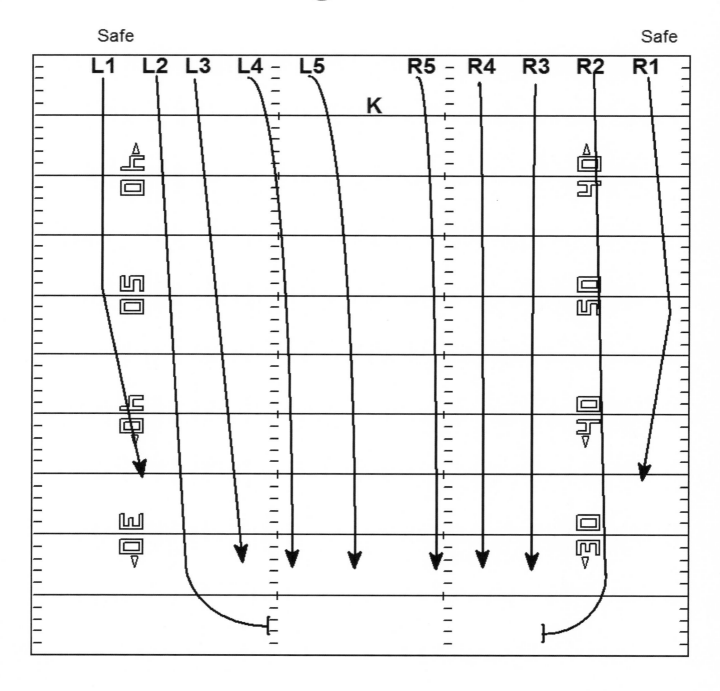

Seattle Kickoff Return

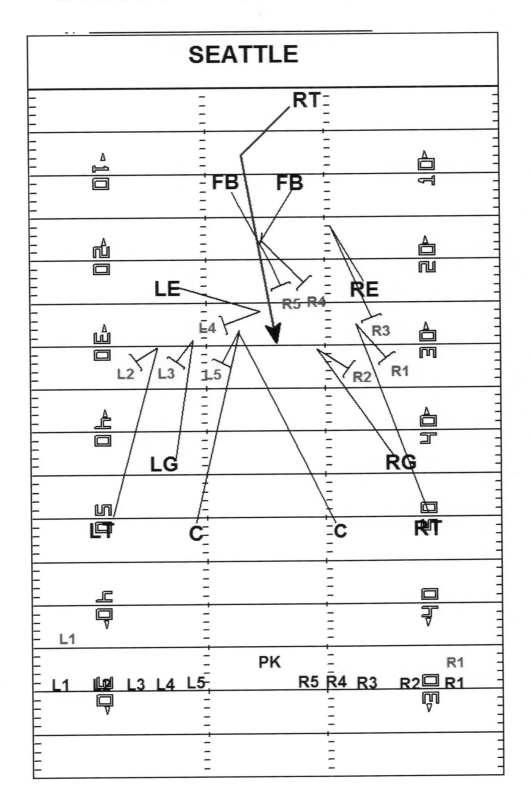

Seattle Drive 5 / Play 1 / 1ˢᵗ & 10 / -20 Yard Line / Middle / 0:31 2Q

NE – 14 SEA – 7

Summary

Gain of 19 yards by Turbin on the carry up the middle for a first down

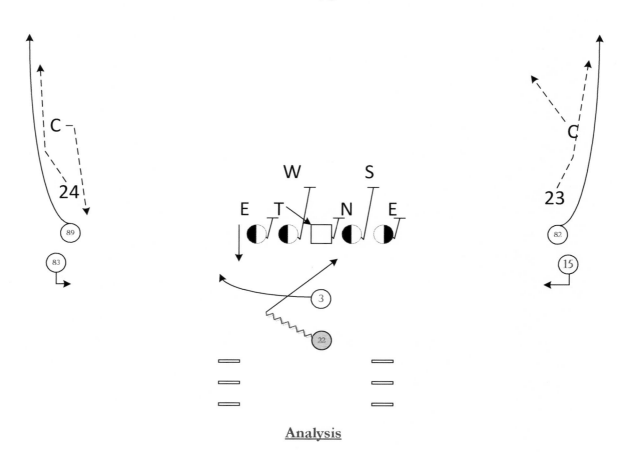

Analysis

This is a pretty low-risk, high-reward situation for Seattle. They're going to go with the conservative play call of handing the ball off to Turbin and see what happens. If he's stuffed on the run, it's unlikely that New England is going to call a time out to force a punt where they'd get the ball back with only 5-10 seconds of time left anyway. Seattle will receive the kickoff to start the 3rd quarter, so Pete Carroll may feel like he's playing with house money here.

Seattle lines up in a formation they've shown several times throughout the season. Two receivers stacked on either side out past the numbers, which provides Wilson (in theory) with a hitch/pitch option on the edge if he decides to take off with the football on the read. This formation also does the job of clearing out the picture for the offensive line and Wilson by opening up the alley to either side and reducing the number of men in the box.

This time, offensive coordinator Darrell Bevell is really attempting to get Russell Wilson matched up on Jamie Collins, while playing formation games with the interior of the defensive front to see how they like to line up and set their strength, since up to this point he's still flying a little bit blind, not having too many opportunities in the first half to give the defense a lot of different looks.

Dont'a Hightower gets pinned to the outside as the left tackle climbs to the second level, and since the defensive tackle to that side is slanting into the A-gap already, he's easy to wash down and the running lane appears.

As a result, Turbin cuts the ball up the field just to the left of the center, and creates a huge play and a lot of momentum for Seattle.

Seattle Drive 5 / Play 2 / 1ˢᵗ & 10 / -39 Yard Line / Left Hash / 0:24 2Q

NE – 14 SEA – 7

Summary

Gain of 16 yards and a first down by Russell Wilson on the zone read keeper to the left.

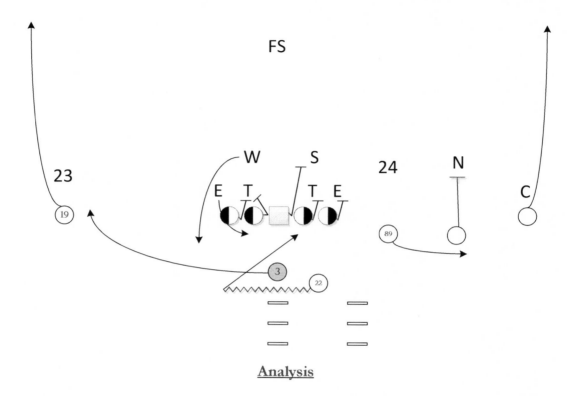

Analysis

Both teams are coming out of a timeout. An interesting note for offensive coordinator Darrell Bevell as he's talking to the offensive assistants on the sideline is that the last play was the first time they've run the zone play with the back off-set to the left side, reading the DE (Jones) to that side. On the previous play, Bevell was trying to get the back to the same side as Jamie Collins the inside linebacker, the Will in this case. He wants to test the option responsibilities to the opposite side of the defense, since up to this point Dont'a Hightower has always been the playside inside linebacker on zone runs.

In other words, whether it's a left/right factor or a strong/weak factor, New England is playing their defensive ends differently to different sides, at least in this balanced front they've played for most of the game, and there may be an opportunity for Russell Wilson to keep it around the edge.

Wilson is quicker than anyone to the left side of the tackle box, so he has the natural athletic advantage, and can avoid any big hits if it doesn't play out exactly the way he thinks. Of course, he's just going to read the end man on the line, so if Jones comes way up the field, Wilson can always just hand it off up the middle as normal.

At the snap, Jones is unblocked on the left side, and Wilson goes through the normal mesh between him and Lynch. Jones comes hard down the line, meaning Wilson will keep the ball. The Will linebacker Collins comes off at the proper angle, nearly boxing the QB into the pocket again, but Wilson gives him just enough of a juke move to shake him, which opens up a huge lane in the left alley. Wilson takes off for a huge gain, and now Seattle is nearly in field goal range.

Seattle Drive 5 / Play 3 / 1ˢᵗ & 10 / +45 Yard Line / Left Hash / 0:17 2Q

NE – 14 SEA – 7

Summary

Pass incomplete intended for Chris Matthews down the deep right half of the field.

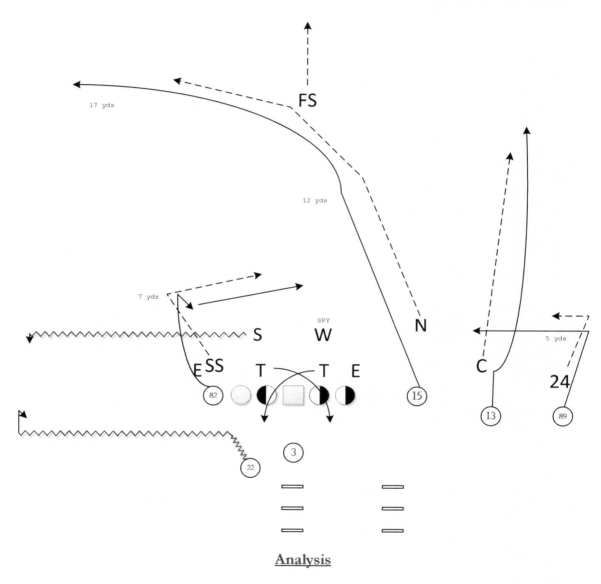

Analysis

Seattle takes a shot down the field to one of their biggest receivers, Chris Matthews, after watching the drop and movement of the FS McCourty. The deep crossing route coming over the top of the TE Wilson's short route clears out any underneath coverage.

Wilson is initially looking to throw Kearse's deep crossing route, since even though the FS McCourty is leaning more toward the left side of the field, he has no real leverage on the route, and there are no threats underneath who could drop and undercut the passing windows for the route.

As Wilson is about to set his feet and throw, he's flushed out of the pocket to the right. When the back Robert Turbin motions out of the backfield out wide, Hightower runs with him, and the offense creates an empty set.

As a result, Jamie Collins moves over the top of the center, and the two defensive tackles go into a twist stunt to control the middle of the offensive line and keep Wilson from running up the middle.

As he's rolling to his right, he sees Chris Matthews one-on-one going down the field and takes a shot.

Seattle Drive 5 / Play 4 / 2ⁿᵈ & 10 / +45 Yard Line / 0:11 2Q

NE – 14 SEA – 7

Summary

Pass complete to Ricardo Lockette down the deep left sideline for a gain of 23 yards and a first down. (A facemask penalty was added on to the end of the play as well.)

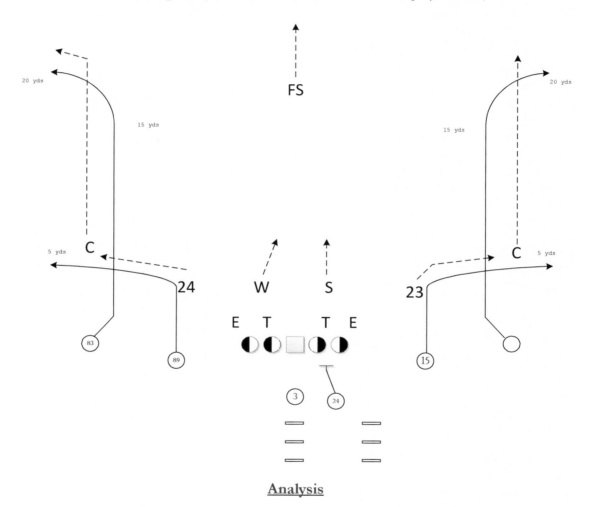

Analysis

With only eleven seconds left on the clock, Seattle has time for only one or two shots down the field, maybe to score the TD, but at the very least get into field goal range. Kicker Steven Hauschka's long in 2014 was 58 yards, so to get within that range, but realistically Pete Carroll wants to get much closer so he doesn't have to rely on his kicker hitting a 58 yarder.

With 2 timeouts remaining, you might think that Seattle has the ability to attack the middle of the field, but the time left is a huge factor, and any deep pass over the middle could take up extra time, especially if there is a potential for yards after the catch. There's also the fact that the Patriots have done a good job of taking away the middle of the field this game so it limits the options the offense has at this point, and you don't want to waste precious seconds taking a low-percentage shot down the field that has next to no chance.

Another factor in quick-strike plays like these is that there isn't a lot of time to go through a complicated progression, so you pretty much have to make your decision before the snap. Wilson takes the snap, eyes the FS for a moment to hold him in the middle of the field, then fires it to Ricardo Lockette deep left down the sideline on the out route. A facemask penalty tacks on several more yards, and suddenly the Seahawks are on the doorstep.

Seattle Drive 5 / Play 5 / 1ˢᵗ & Goal / +10 Yard Line / Left Hash / 0:06 2Q

NE – 14 SEA – 7

Summary

Touchdown! Pass complete to Chris Matthews for a ten yard gain near the left pylon and a score.

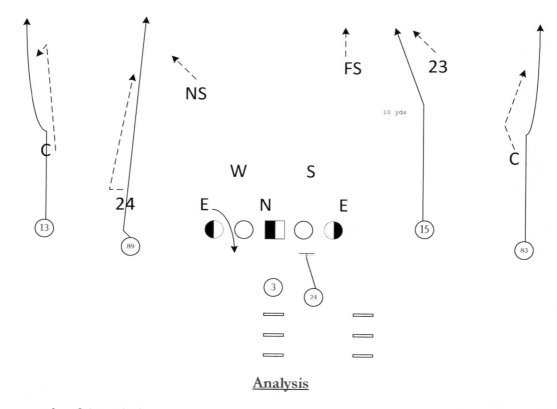

Analysis

This is an example of 4 verticals which is one of the simplest plays to draw up, but underneath that simple exterior is a large amount of complexity.

The basic strategy in this part of the field is that you want to get the ball to your biggest guy on the outside, throw it up to a place where only he can get it, and let him use his size and athleticism to do what he does best. With only 6 seconds left, this has to be a "catch-and-throw" situation from Wilson. As we talked about on the last play, these is no time to drop back and survey the whole field waiting for the coverage to develop. Wilson knows where he's going before the play even starts.

The Patriots defense is concerned with defending the middle of the field, which is why the two safeties are aligned inside of the slot receivers, so Wilson knows that the vertical routes by the inside receivers will hold the safeties in place, and free up the outside receivers. Since he's on the left hash, the throw to Matthews on the left side is even closer than Lockette to the right, so that's where he decides to go. The route is a pretty simple one for Matthews. The corner across from him, Logan Ryan, is backpedaling from the start in order to defend against a fade route that he knows is coming. Matthews however begins to peek inside once he gets past the 1st five yards and sees the ball coming out of Wilson's hand headed toward the front pylon, so he throttles his route down, and opens inward to shield the defender from the football before making the catch just as he crosses the goal line.

Seattle PAT / New England PAT Block

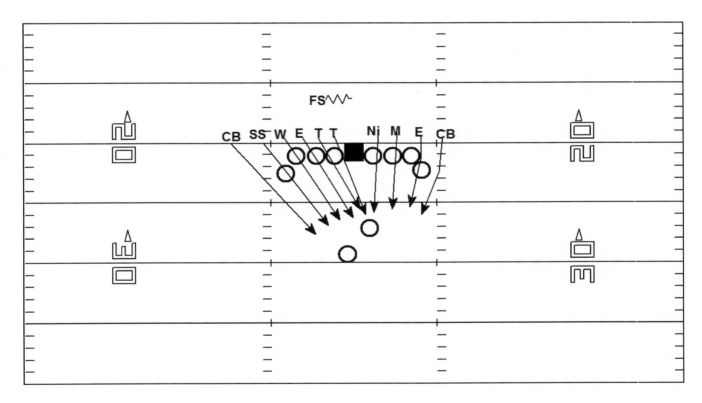

Seattle Kickoff

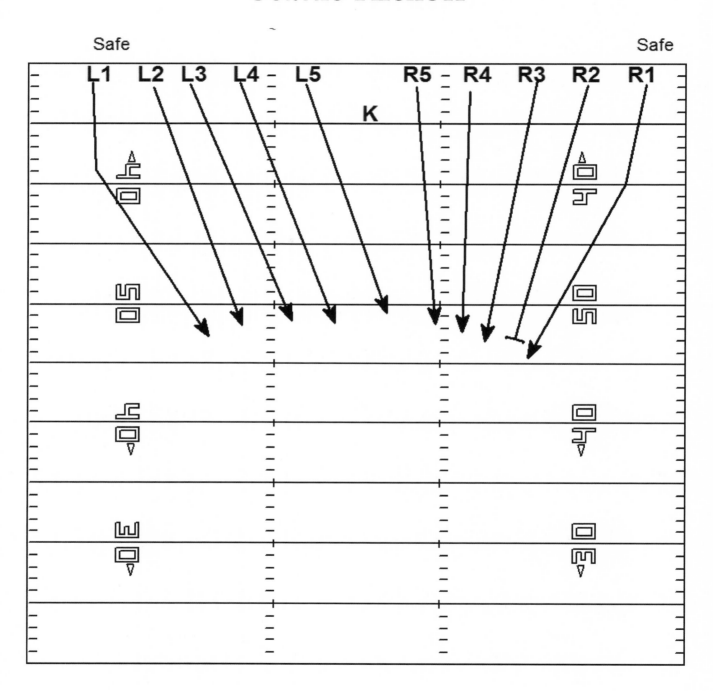

New England Kickoff Return

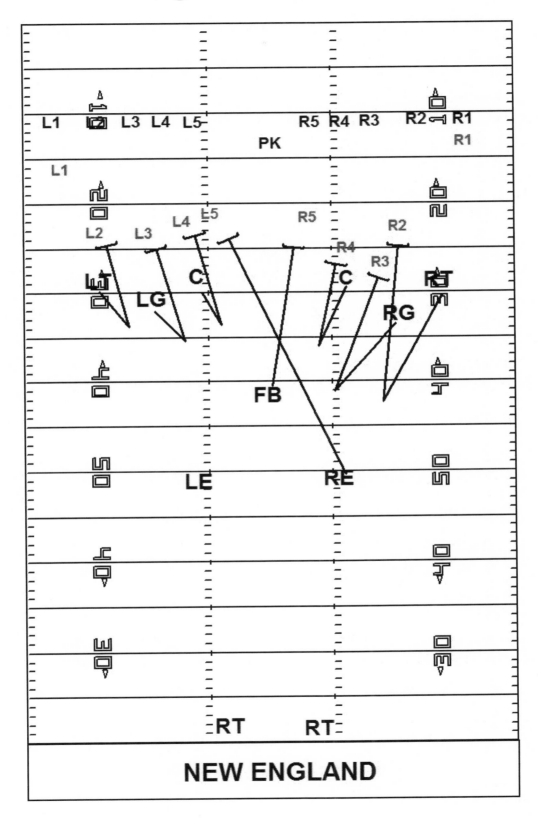

Seattle Drive #5 Review

This is a pretty low-risk/ high-reward situation for Seattle. They've got a few tricks up their sleeve to try and get into scoring position, but they're also getting the ball to start the 2nd half as well, so Pete Carroll is basically playing with house money at this point.

Bevell has a quandary to start the drive. He wants to get down the field and into scoring position, but he doesn't want to just throw a long incompletion, because then Seattle is in a hole on 2nd and 10. While New England wouldn't call a timeout after a short run up the middle that keeps the clock moving under 30 seconds, they'd still take the opportunity to make Seattle punt if it's suddenly 2nd and 10 with the clock stopped. After that happens it's basically a way of attrition, as Seattle would hope to pick up 10 yards on the ground in 2 plays, otherwise New England could use both their remaining timeouts and for the Seahawks to punt.

It's worth mentioning that New England may not have any intention of getting the football back and heaving a pass toward the end zone as time expires, but there is value in forcing your opponent to punt deep inside his own territory. For one, there's always the possibility for a great return to set up a score but also because there's the possibility of a fumbled snap, blocked punt, or an otherwise botched play. Ask any coach who's been in the game long enough, and they've all got at least one story about the time they were screwed on a bad special teams play that was supposed to be routine.

Back to the situation at hand, Bevell wants to move the ball in a hurry on the ground, but there's no guarantee Lynch can break free up the middle, so he's going to try to manufacture a big play from Russell Wilson on the zone read.

But how?

As we've said before, the defensive ends have been playing up the field all day long, and the defense has been designed to keep Wilson in the pocket, even if he tries to run the zone read.

The thing is, this is exactly why Bevel has been throwing so many different looks at the defense during the game. Like a scientist running experiments and trying to find answers, Bevell went into the game with some questions. As the game has progressed, he's answered some of them, and he's got a couple of theories, now it's time to test them out.

Up to this point, Seattle has not attempted to run any zone read plays or any kind of zone runs where they leave the weak side defensive end unblocked. By weak side, I mean away from the passing strength, since a couple of times already Seattle has lined up with the TE split out all by himself to one side like a receiver.

So the Seahawks are going to try to run the zone read to the opposite side for the first time in the game, and see if they're playing the defensive end any differently.

What he doesn't realize at this point is that the option responsibilities in this front has as much to do with defensive personnel as they do with the strength of the formation. Basically what it means is that the inside linebacker to each side determines the option responsibilities with Hightower #54 almost always lining up to the strong side and Collins #91 almost always lining up to the weak side.

Bill Belichick is famous for simplifying things for his players while giving the illusion of complexity. In keeping with that theme, he's giving his two primary inside linebackers only one responsibility each, one (Hightower) is the guy who will crash the A-gap, and the other LB (Collins) is the guy who will either come from the backside as the bonus guy on the run play, or will be the "scraper" responsible for the QB on zone read plays if the DE to his side is the one left unblocked.

In the case of this first play, Bevel wants to create as much space to the outside for Wilson to use, and he assumes that without a TE in a balanced 2x2 set like this one, they'll set the strength to their left since so far this offense has been pretty right-handed in the game so far.

Normally he'd be right, but in this situation the defense has a stunt called. The DT lined up over the left guard is assigned to slant into the A-gap and play as the 1-technique as if he'd been lined up there the whole time.

The called slant allows the LG to wash him down very easily on the play, pushing him out of the way, and Hightower doesn't quite fit correctly in his gap, which allows Lynch to break free for a big gain and a 1st down.

Basically what happened on their first play is that Seattle was expecting one look from the defense, but got another, and got very lucky when they called the right play for the defensive scheme that had been called.

But what about the next play? Bevell still wants to get the ball in Wilson's hands somehow, and he still has the same idea.

This time on the 2nd play, he gets the offense to line up in a 3x1 set with no TE on the field, and even the back Robert Turbin is aligned to the right before flipping sides. This was done to ensure that Hightower would line up to the right because there would be no doubt where the strength of the formation is. In this way, Bevell can be sure he's attacking the weak side of the defense, and that he'll get the look he wants.

This time, Bevel's plans work out perfectly. The DE Chandler Jones closes down the line off the "give" and Wilson takes off around the corner, narrowly escaping the grip of ILB Jamie Collins, the player responsible for the QB in the option. Now there's plenty of open space in the weak side alley for Wilson to run through, and he suddenly has the offense close to scoring range.

Three plays later the offense scores, courtesy of a nice throw from Wilson to Chris Matthews near the left pylon, but the most interesting part of the drive occurred during the first two plays. How will Belichick adjust, and will Bevel be able to take what he's learned and use it effectively? The offense will be back on the field in the 3rd quarter, so he'd better figure things out in a hurry.

Seattle Halftime Review - Offense

Y-Off -

There is a lot of room for big plays in the pass game out of this alignment, particularly on 1st down. New England brought in some extra bodies to play against the run during the 1st half once the Seattle offense really got moving on their first scoring drive.

One overlooked version of the Y-off alignment comes in the form of the bunch formation. This offensive set allows Seattle to get good angles to the strong side in the run game, create natural rubs for their receivers in the pass game, and bring the tight end back across to the weak side in the run game on the wham play.

It also creates the opportunity for a lot of play action and boot concepts to throw the ball down the field, since the vertical passing game is one of the few areas where this offense has been successful so far tonight.

Outside Pass Routes -

New England has made it absolutely clear that they are not going to allow Russell Wilson any easy throws. By crowding the box against the run and playing a whole lot of robber with a safety playing intermediate depth in the middle of the field taking away the digs and crossing routes and any other high-percentage throws that could serve to help keep Russell Wilson's offense moving forward on schedule.

The tight man coverage being played across the board by New England, as well as the assignment by Revis on Baldwin means that offensive coordinator Darrell Bevell can basically place New England's best corner wherever he wants on the field. Most importantly, he can be assured that Revis is removed from the area of the field he intends to attack.

The vertical passes Seattle completed late in the 1st half likely hold the key to their continued offensive success in the 2nd half.

Inside Zone against a covered center –

By now, Seattle must have recognized New England's plan of attack, realizing that Bill Belichick wants to keep an inside linebacker free to pursue the ball carrier untouched by the offensive line. However as Bevell no doubt noticed on the final drive before halftime, New England's inside linebackers have a tendency to come downhill very aggressively, sometimes so quickly that they end up missing their run fits. The first play of Seattle's final drive in the first half is proof enough of that, since it was the combination of Hightower and Collins poor run fits that sprang Lynch loose for a big play up the middle and set the stage for the tying score.

If Lynch can be just a tiny bit more patient in the backfield, helping to set up his blocker and bringing the linebackers closer to his offensive line, there is a lot of potential for big plays in the second half.

Seattle Halftime Review - Defense

Take away the middle of the field –

When we talk about taking away the middle of the field, it's not so much that we're trying to plant a defender in the center of the field between the two hash marks, and whose assignment consists entirely of knocking off any offensive player crossing the middle, though there are plenty of coaches out there who use this strategy.

When we talk about taking away the middle of the field, what we're really talking about in this case is that we want to take away the specific route (the shallow cross by Edelman) from roaming free over the middle, and just as importantly, limiting the yards after the catch.

Seattle has used a couple of different strategies to this end, including playing some robber coverages that force all in-breaking routes into the middle where a safety or linebacker is waiting to pounce. This will be crucial in the second half.

Defend the single receiver side -

The single receiver side of the formation and the left side of the formation have often been one and the same in the first half for New England, doing their best to attack the coverage away from Richard Sherman's side of the field.

Seattle has alternated between press coverage and bracket coverage when the receiver is aligned in a tight split off the left tackle. At the moment, the Patriots have shown all kinds of ways to attack that side of the field, and with the loss of Jeremy Lane for the rest of the game, the defensive backs for Seattle are becoming rarer and rarer, and Tharold Simon will have to pick up a lot of the slack.

Limit Vereen's ability to do damage out of the backfield -

Part of this goes back to what we talked about in the pre-game notes, and the importance of flying to the football and gang-tackling once the ball is caught.

It's next to impossible to prevent a running back from catching the football out of the backfield, but it's very important to get a defender on him the minute he does catch the ball to limit his yards after the catch.

If Seattle can limit Vereen's effectiveness, that will help stop Edelman from running free across the middle on the shallow crossing route, and take away a big part of New England's offensive game plan.

New England Halftime Review - Offense

Find new ways to get Gronkowski the football-

As that final play for New England proved, tight end Rob Gronkowski is a huge threat to the defense wherever he is on the field, and can even go deep when called upon to do so. Seattle's decision to line a linebacker up against Gronk on the last play of the half came back to haunt them, but it's likely that New England can do much more with Gronk in the passing game, and given the matchup problems he presents to defenses based on just his size, it's in the Patriots' best interest to move around as much as possible to force the defense to adjust and put them in an uncomfortable situation.

So far New England has used Gronk in so many different ways in the first half, both as a receiver and as a blocker. Coming out of halftime, they need to force Seattle to account for Gronkowski in pass coverage.

Continue to get the ball to Vereen out of the backfield-

Yes it's true that the Patriots have the goal of creating open spaces for the shallow crossing route by Edelman, but before that can happen, Vereen must make himself a credible threat out of the backfield, which he has managed to do brilliantly so far in this game.

Vereen has gotten open out of the backfield, as well as lining up out wide on occasion.

The real reason Vereen is so important to the success of the shallow cross is that the defenders planted in the middle of the field responsible for taking away the underneath routes of the receivers is one less guy they can commit to stopping Vereen's pass routes out of the backfield. Once they decide to pick their poison, whether that's to stop the shallow route or the backfield routes, then New England can dictate this phase of the game.

Use LaFell and Amendola to pick on Tharold Simon

Since Jeremy Lane went down after the interception of Tom Brady, #27 Tharold Simon comes on the field as the nickel corner, and so far he's been the most vulnerable of the three corners that Seattle has played with. As much as New England is attacking the left side, particularly when playing with compressed formations and 3x1 sets with the single receiver set to the left side, Simon is going to be a factor in this game and in the Patriots game plan whether he likes it or not.

Part of the Patriots first drive or two should be dedicated to figuring out how, if at all, Seattle will re-shuffle their secondary or coverage schemes with Simon in. During the first half at least, there was no noticeable difference. It's likely that Pete Carroll and Dan Quinn won't make many changes at all.

New England Halftime Review - Defense

Y-Off-

One of the consistent features of a Bill Belichick-coached defense over the years is that the defensive front is not tied to whatever the guys in the secondary are doing.

For much of the 1st half, New England's defensive front is aligned in a balanced look, with equal numbers on both sides of the center, and whose alignments are almost exactly the same regardless of whether or not there is a tight end in the box. In the nickel package for instance, the strong safety Patrick Chung is responsible for going with the tight end no matter where he is, responsible for covering him when he runs a route downfield, and also responsible for controlling the edge in the run game outside of the tight end. Add to that the technique of the defensive ends Chandler Jones and Rob Ninkovich play up the field when unblocked most of the time which can help take away any jet sweep action.

These are the reasons why New England shouldn't have to work too hard to make adjustments, since on paper they've got answers for everything, including the counter play that Seattle ran with some success earlier, without changing up what they're already doing.

Much of the coaching in the locker room involves reaffirming the plan that has been put in place, eliminating the tendency to hesitate when being given a jet sweep fake or another false key, and just focus on the simple steps they've been given and have been practicing for the past two weeks.

Five-Man Surface-

This kind of formation was obviously instrumental on the final drive, creating space in the alley for Russell Wilson to take off around the edge that created such a huge play. The Patriots must create a better edge to both sides of the formation, and give the defense a numbers advantage in the box, playing the run aggressively until Seattle proves they can be effective throwing the football out of this alignment.

Create balanced fronts vs all personnel groups-

It's important to remember that the whole idea behind Belichick's game plan is to plug up the interior line, covering up both guards and the center. At the same time, certain offensive personnel groups lend themselves toward specific formations more than others.

As we talked about on the 2nd drive for example, when Seattle first brings on 13 personnel, New England is expecting a much different look from the offense. As a result, the Patriots end up in an under front that forces the Sam linebacker to split the difference between the slot receiver Kearse and the tight end Luke Wilson instead of allowing him to play up on the line of scrimmage where he would have less to worry about. (Why Seattle didn't take advantage of the mis-match in the passing game with a big tall receiver lined up across from a linebacker who was out of place is a bit of a mystery, but I digress.)

By removing the Sam linebacker from the box, and forcing the defense to create an open B gap to a formation they would've normally played a more balanced look to, Seattle forced New England to limit the number of defensive fronts they could call against personnel groups like this one, since Belichick has no way of knowing whether the offense will align in a one-back set or a more traditional two-back formation that lends itself to the power run game. It also opens up more room for the run off-tackle, since the Patriots are now more concerned with keeping the interior linemen covered up than securing the C gap, and as a result the Seahawks can have more success in that area, like on play #8 of the 4th drive when the offense lined up in twins and inserted the fullback into the C gap on the strong safety.

The Patriots may have fewer fronts to choose from, but they still have a good amount of flexibility in terms of personnel within the fronts that they can still run. They have the ability to play a similar "bear" front out of their base nickel package that still occupies the interior offensive linemen, keeps the inside linebacker free, and gets more bodies in pass defense for the Patriots.

If Belichick can stay flexible and the Patriot defenders can do their jobs and win their individual matchups, it will go a long way toward a successful 2nd half and winning the game.

New England Kickoff

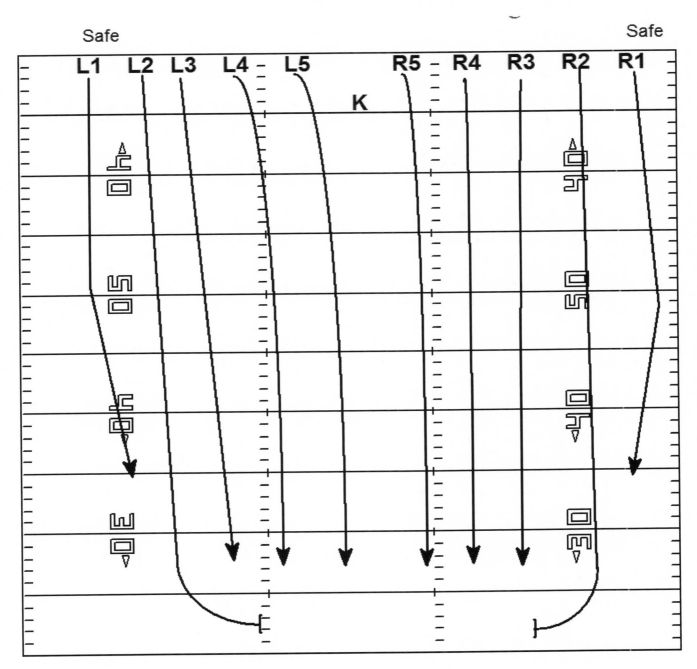

Seattle Kickoff

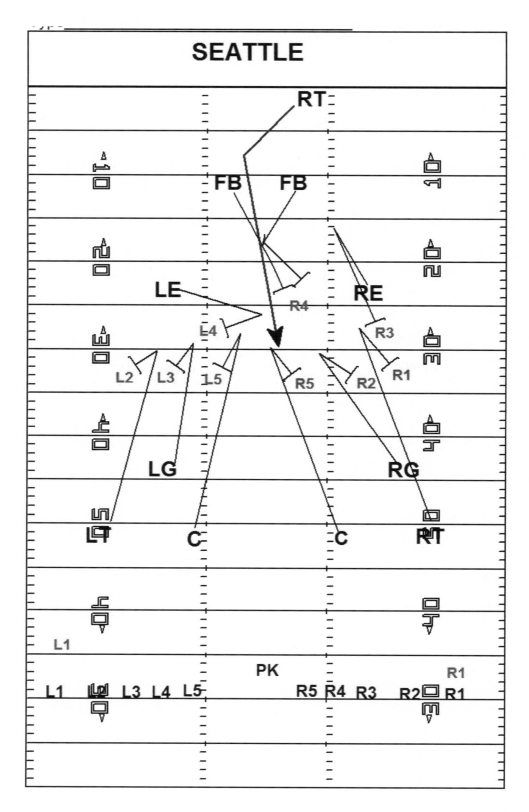

Seattle Drive 6 / Play 1 / 1ˢᵗ & 10 / -20 Yard Line / Middle / 15:00 3Q

NE – 14 SEA – 14

Summary

Gain of 4 yards up the middle.

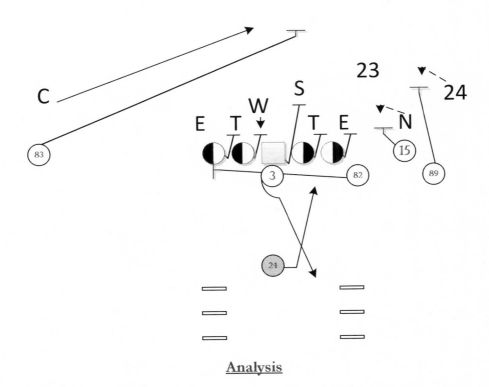

Analysis

The Seattle offense comes out of the locker room with a formation and play call that combines many of the most successful parts of their offense from the first half.

The Y-off package that Darrell Bevel put together works will with this 11 personnel and the bunch formation that they've already tried a couple of times.

The New England defense, meanwhile, comes with a little bit of a change up, with the Will linebacker Collins lining up right over the top of the center, and shoots through the left A-gap leaving Hightower as the free linebacker. Belichick decided to bring an adjusted blitz packaged on this play to keep the offense off-balance, but Lynch still manages to pick up four yards.

Seattle Drive 6 / Play 2 / 2nd & 6 / -23 Yard Line / Right Hash / 14:40 3Q

NE 14 – SEA – 14

Summary

Gain of 25 yards on the carry up the middle by Lynch.

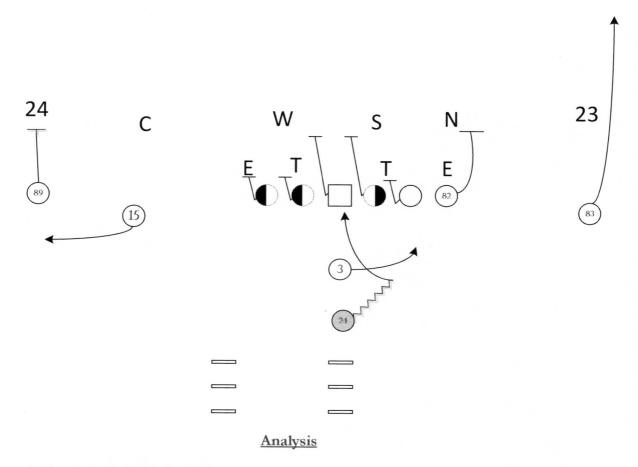

Analysis

There are mistakes by both inside linebackers on this play.

On the play, the Will linebacker actually vacates his position on the left side when trying to come over the top from the backside to help on the front side of the play. The place where the Will linebacker used to stand is exactly where Lynch ends up breaking.

However, the Sam (Hightower) doesn't get across the to the opposite A gap like he's supposed to, which means that the Will linebacker isn't in the right gap. When the Will (Collins) comes over the top to the other side, the center's job is so much easier, all he has to do is take Collins where he wants to go.

Seattle Drive 6 / Play 3 / 1ˢᵗ & 10 / -38 Yard Line / Left Hash / 14:00 3Q

NE – 14 SEA – 14

Summary

Pass completed to Chris Matthews for a gain of 45 yards and a first down deep down the sideline.

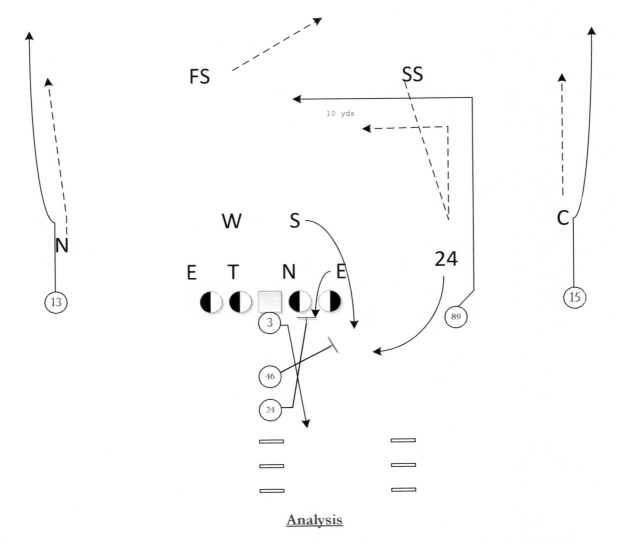

Analysis

The depth of the dig route by the slot receiver over the middle, combined with the play action fake is designed to open up space in the middle, and the receiver should be deep enough so that the underneath coverage is not in a great position to undercut any in-breaking routes over the middle.

Seattle has decided that they want to take another shot on 1st down, and offensive coordinator Darrelle Bevell has wisely placed Doug Baldwin is the slot, so that no matter which vertical route opens up down the field depending on the rotation of the secondary, they won't have to compete against the Patriots' best cover man in Revis.

Revis actually comes off the slot position to blitz off the edge in this situation along with the Sam linebacker, which leaves the SS Patrick Chung manned up or Baldwin over the middle. As Wilson comes out of his play fake and sets up 8 yards deep in the backfield, he takes a quick look at the FS then fires deep down the left side when Matthews is running step-for-step with the corner and #25 Kyle Arrington and makes a great leaping grab down the sideline for a huge play.

Seattle Drive 6 / Play 4 / 1st & 10 / +17 Yard Line / Left Hash / 13:30 3Q

NE – 14 SEA – 14

Summary

Gain of 7 yards by Lynch on the carry to the left side.

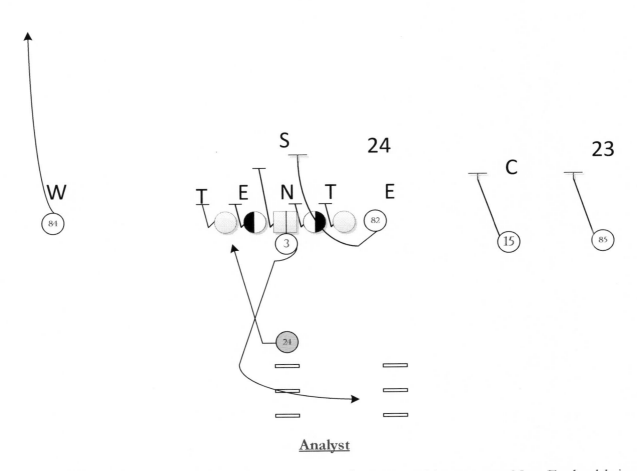

Analyst

Seattle brings on their 13 personnel on 1st down (3 TE/ 1 RB), and in response New England brings in their heavy package with an extra defensive tackles to help with the run game. Like most teams, Belichick's defense is heavily reliant on paying attention to the offensive personnel coming on to the field, since it's a huge indicator of what the offense plans to do.

Due to the unique offensive personnel package on the field, Revis gets pulled into the box to align over the top of the TE #82 Luke Wilson, since he's now over one of the best receivers on the field. Wilson ends up wrapping around the backside tackle (who is cutting Wilfork), thanks to the angles on the backside of the play, and comes up to the 2nd level through the B-gap.

Now the offense is in 2nd and 3 and in great position to go ahead in scoring position.

Seattle Drive 6 / Play 5 / 2nd & 3 / +10 Yard Line / Left Hash / 12:49 3Q

NE – 14 SEA – 14

Summary

A gain of 2 yards by Lynch on the carry up the middle.

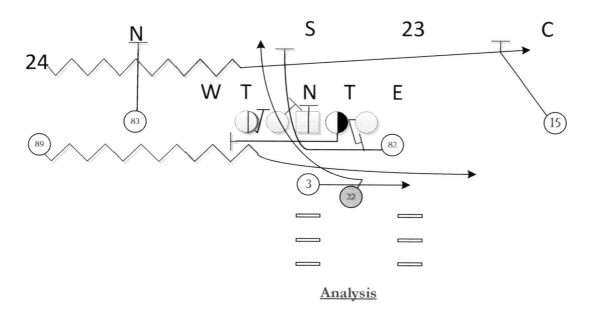

Analysis

Lynch comes off the field on the play, and Robert Turbin takes his place in the backfield next to Wilson.

Chandler Jones is playing head up over the left tackle, who is responsible for winning on the front side edge. Jones sheds the block almost immediately off the snap, and forces the ball back to the inside. As a result, the Sam linebacker ends up unblocked, and the play hits tight enough so that the nose can come over the top of the down block and get his hands on the runner.

Doug Baldwin comes in motion across the formation as if he's about to take the handoff, and he takes Revis with him. The play picks up 2 yards, even with the penetration into the backfield, and sets up a crucial 3rd and 1.

This is the opposite situation of the previous play, where the offensive personnel provides a key to the play call that's coming. Seattle takes their best runner off the field and brings on 3 receivers. It's a pass play, right? Wrong.

Darrelle Bevell tries to catch New England off-guard, and the offense nearly picks up the 1st down, but is stopped short.

Seattle Drive 6 / Play 6 / 3rd & 1 / +8 Yard Line / Left Hash / 12:14 3Q

NE – 14 SEA – 14

Summary

Lynch is stopped at the line of scrimmage for no gain.

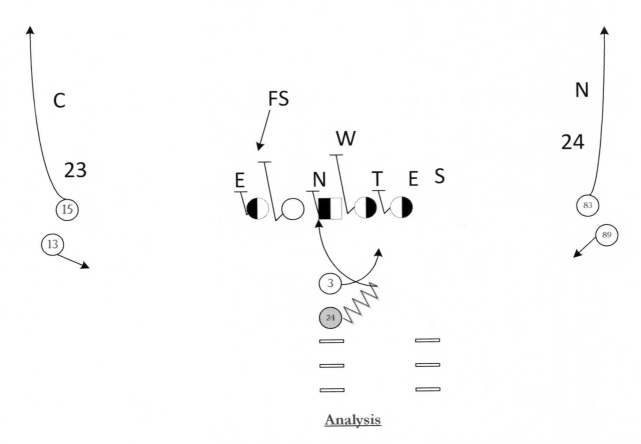

Analysis

Here's another situation where Seattle lines up in the pistol and picks a side in the zone run game, in this example they're running the wide zone because of the edge pressure showing pre-snap from the right side.

The aiming point of Lynch is so tight to the middle of the formation that Ninkovich is able to come off the edge in a hurry and grab a hold of him before he's able to pick up a 1st down.

McCourty the FS is aligned down low over the B gap, but for some reason the LG doesn't locate him, so that he comes off his combos he's looking to the right instead of locating McCourty coming downhill. So the FS comes unblocked into the gap and helps stop Lynch before he picks up the 1st down.

Seattle FG / New England FG Block

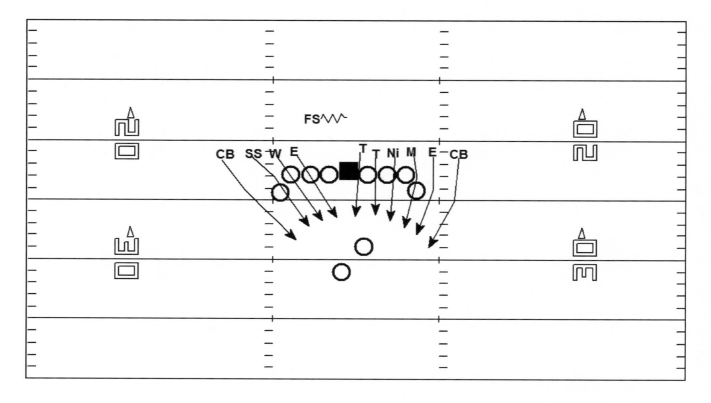

Seattle Drive #6 Review

Seattle opens the 3nd half in a bunch formation. Though they did try to use the bunch earlier in the game, the play was blown dead because of a false start so Darrell Bevell never got a good look at how the defense responded to it. Also, the personnel to the side of the bunch has been changed, with the TE off the line playing the inside man in the bunch instead of on the point.

As we talked about at the beginning of the game, having Lynch in the backfield gives the offensive coaching staff a kind of carte blanche to experiment with different alignments, knowing they'll be able to pick up a few yards based on Lynch's talents alone.\\

The rest of the drive is a rehashing of formations and plays that worked for Seattle in the first half, which allows Bevel to see how NE has adjusted, if at all, to the looks on offense he liked the most.

New England made a couple of changes to their alignment on a couple of plays, including coming out with more "bear" looks up front that covered up all three interior linemen, and provided a much more balanced look so that Seattle couldn't line up and run it at the open B-gap which they tried to do earlier in the game.

The defense is also much more aggressive against the same 2x2 formation that Seattle had success with during the final drive, putting the Sam linebacker up on the line and stacking Collins nearby over the top of the nose, in a position to roam around since the guys upfront should be able to keep the blockers off of him.

The defense gives a similar look to the same Y-off formations that Seattle used to run the counter play in the 1st half, and they do again, only this time the play is held to just a 2 yard gain.

Bevell has found a few formations he likes, and he wants to find out as soon as possible how Belichick plans to defend them, so that he can go to work on devising adjustments of his own.

Seattle Kickoff

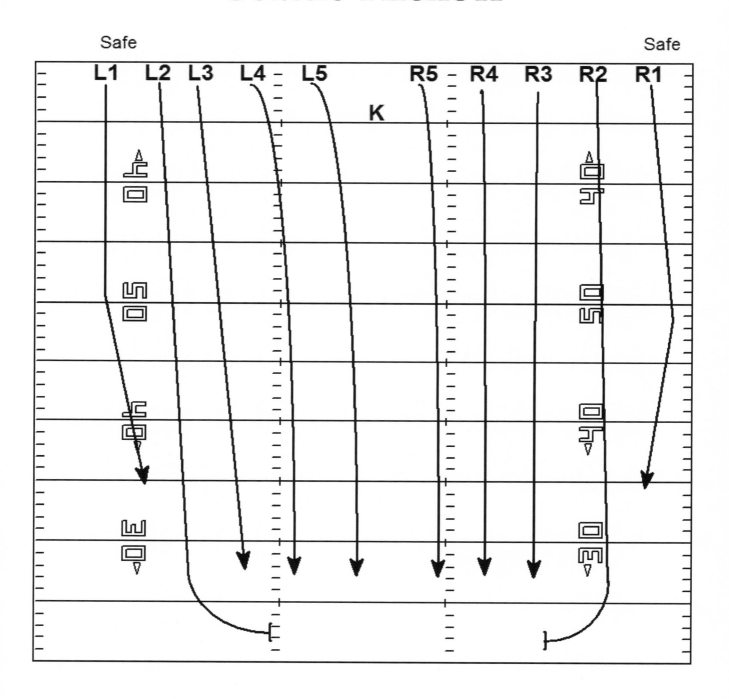

New England Kickoff Return

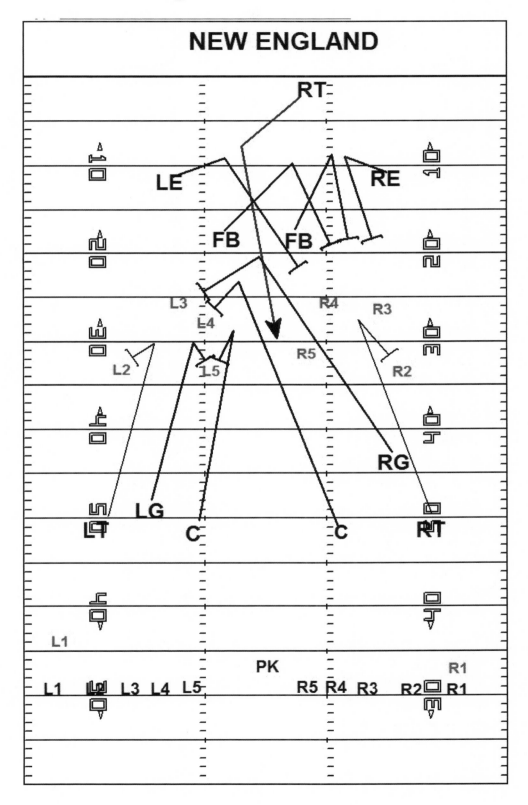

New England Drive 6 / Play 1 / 1ˢᵗ & 10 / -20 Yard Line / Left Hash / 11:09 3Q

NE – 14 SEA – 17

Summary

Pass complete to Edelman in the left flat for a gain of 3 yards.

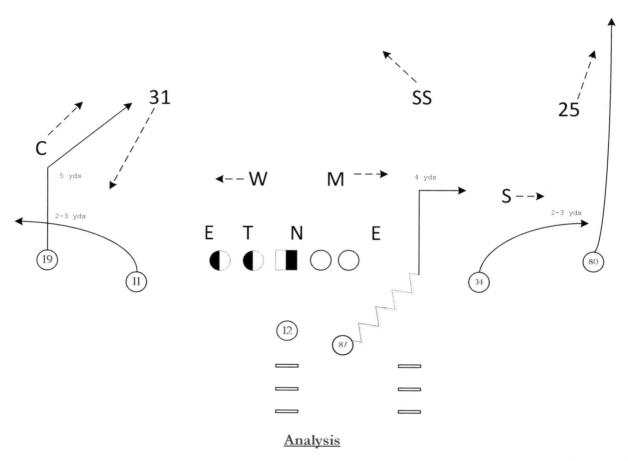

Analysis

Brady points out the Will linebacker for the offensive line, which slides that way, and then sends Gronk in motion out of the backfield to pull the Mike out of the box or at least provide a hot receiver in case the Mike blitzes.

It's a pretty easy read for Brady though, seeing as how Amendola is completely uncovered in the slot to the left pre-snap, with Chancellor aligned deep over him at about an 8-yard depth.

Brady takes the snap and peeks over at the corner to the left side. Since he drops to cover the slant route from LaFell, Brady fires it quickly to Amendola running the flat route to the open space near the sideline, putting New England in great shape for 2nd down.

New England Drive 6 / Play 2 / 2ⁿᵈ & 7 / -23 Yard Line / Left Hash / 10:52 3Q

NE – 14 SEA – 17

Summary

Gain of 1 yard on the run from Blount along the left side.

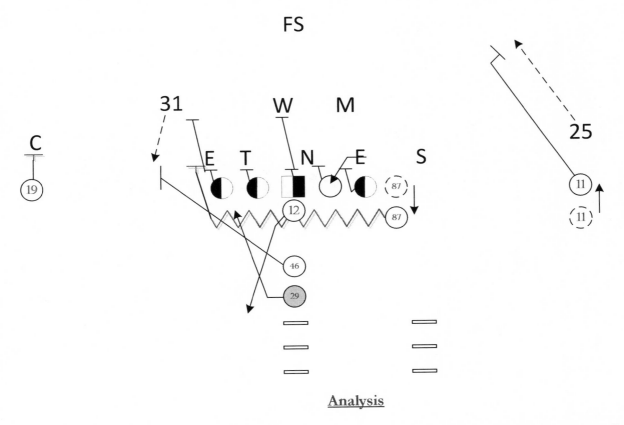

Analysis

Brady doesn't like the picture to the strong side with the angle on the nose tackle. He moves Gronk to the opposite side but Gronk releases his block on the DE and the play is dead.

Using Gronk as the front side guy on this play, especially when you move him around and he has to make split-second decisions and ID the right guy it's not a great idea. Coming out of the half time break, New England is trying to give Seattle a few different looks to break some tendencies, but this play falls short.

New England Drive 6 / Play 3 / 3rd & 6 / -24 Yard Line / Left Hash / 10:10 3Q

NE – 14 SEA – 17

Summary

Pass complete to Gronkowski for a gain of 7 yards and a first down.

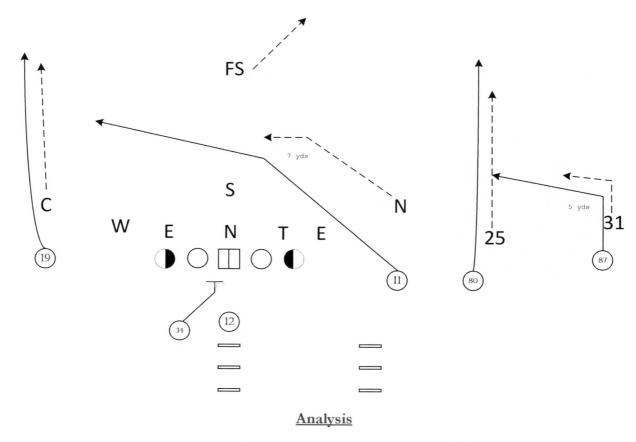

Analysis

Once again we see Gronk split out wide, only this time he's to the 3 WR side of the formation. As a result, the Patriots can use other receivers nearly to clear out any underneath coverage, and since he's matched up against Chancellor on this play, he's definitely facing man coverage, and the vertical route by Amendola taking Sherman out of the picture clears up the passing lane and means that Gronk can catch the ball and get vertical right away with no additional resistance.

The routes are set up so that if Gronk can beat his man inside he's got all kinds of room to make a play after the catch, and that's what he does.

New England Drive 6 / Play 4 / 1st & 10 / -31 Yard Line / Middle / 9:27 3Q

NE – 14 SEA – 17

Summary

Gain of 1 yard on the run to the right by Blount.

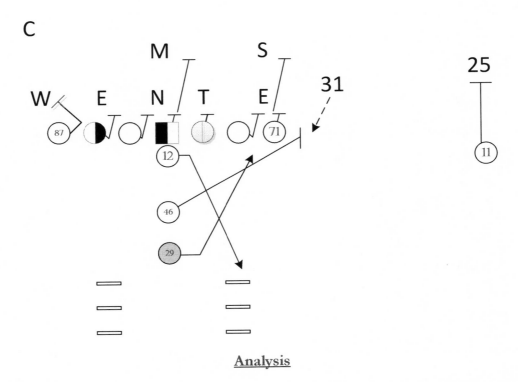

Analysis

It's safe to say that Seattle has the 22 personnel package figured out by this point in the game already, and New England doesn't really have an answer right now.

The nose and backside DE cause enough disruption in the middle of the offensive line which allows he Mike linebacker to roam free to Blount as he tries to cut back. In this situation, Seattle accomplishes their goal of protecting their 2nd-level guys so that they can pursue the ball carrier.

New England needs some kind of pass threat or a constraint play to Gronkowski's side of the formations to free up space for the run game to the strong side.

New England Drive 6 / Play 5 / 2ⁿᵈ & 9 / -32 Yard Line / Right Hash / 8:48 3Q

NE – 14 SEA – 17

Summary

Pass incomplete intended for Gronkowski over the middle.

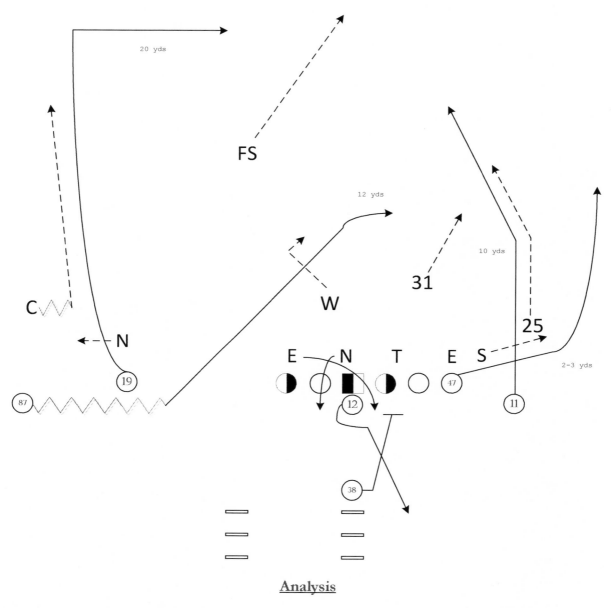

Analysis

The Sam linebacker plays the TE Hoomanawanui man-to-man because of the tight split of the Z receiver, and with Sherman taking on the vertical route, this leaves all kinds of room outside the numbers for the TE to get open behind Sherman.

Brady is nearly sacked on this play when the LDE stunts inside and knocks him down as he's throwing a pass toward Gronkowski that falls painfully short. Regardless the middle was very well defended and there wasn't much room for the pass to begin with.

New England Drive 6 / Play 6 / 3rd & 9 / -32 Yard Line / Right Hash / 8:15 3Q

NE – 14 SEA – 17

Summary

Pass intended for Gronkowski over the middle is intercepted by the Will linebacker #54 Bobby Wagner

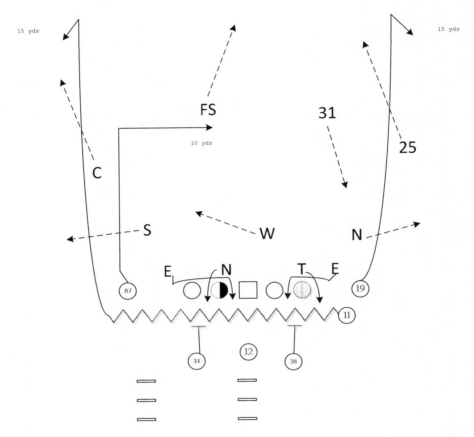

New England sends Edelman in motion from right to left hoping to force the defense to shift and create a situation where Gronkowski or Edelman could create some leverage on their route to that side. It's a "change of strength" motion, which is significant because it will force someone, somewhere on defense to move and ideally create extra space for the offense to exploit.

This is not a great play call to begin with against a defense that has successfully defended the medium-to-deep middle of the field. There is no real underneath threat to stress the defense vertically. And not even a token play fake. The success of the play hinges on the ability of Gronk to use his strength and agility to muscle his way across the middle and find a window to settle down in.

Bobby Wagner does a great job of feeling where the pass would end up, and strong arms his way to the pass as he steps in front of Gronk to pick this one off. The reality is that the play was doomed from the start. It's simply an instance where the Patriots have to admit they were caught in a bad call.

New England Drive #6 Review

Coming out of the locker room at the start of the 3rd quarter, Josh McDaniels has decided to make an effort to get the ball to Gronkowski, and move him around the formation as much as possible and try to force the ball into the middle of the field.

Also of note is that Seattle appears to have adjusted to the 22 personnel tight formation on the outside zone, shutting down anything on the edge for the Patriots.

New England doesn't have much of a run threat at this point in the game, and all it does is make the defensive line for Seattle let loose with the pass rush even more, since Michael Bennett has been a thorn in Tom Brady's side all night with his constant pressure.

Also of note, defensive end Cliff Avril was knocked out of the game on the interception with concussion symptoms, and it is very unlikely he'll return at this point.

Seattle Drive 7 / Play 1 / 1ˢᵗ & 10 / 50 Yard Line / Left Hash / 8:07 3Q

NE – 14 SEA – 17

Summary

Pass complete to Chris Matthews on the hitch route to the left side for a gain of 9 yards.

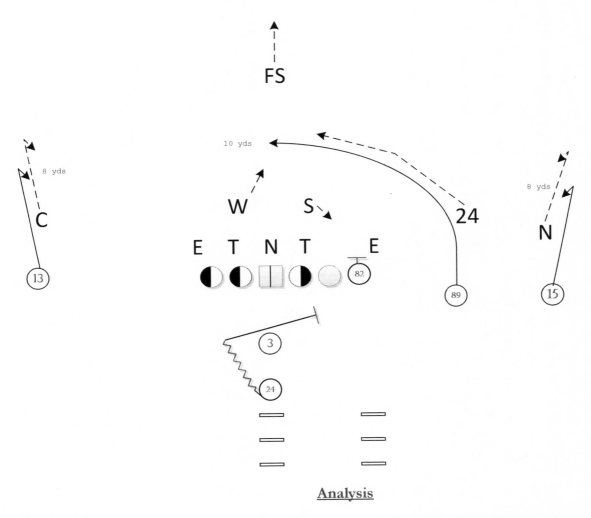

Analysis

Seattle builds off a lot of earlier success with shifting from the pistol and setting Lynch to one side or the other by packaging a play action concept with the same expanding hitch route that they've run successfully several times during the course of the game.

As we've talked about earlier, many times play action is run in order to time up the throw. In this case, Russell Wilson's throwing motion is set up perfectly by carrying out the fake to Lynch and then dropping and resetting his body. Matthews pushes vertical on the corner Brandon Browner #39 in front of him, and actually gets away with what some people might consider offensive pass interference.

The Seahawks have to find several reliable ways to move the football on 1st down, and at least a couple of them have to be pass plays.

Seattle Drive 7 / Play 2 / 2nd & 1 / +41 Yard Line / Left Hash / 7:47 3Q

NE – 14 SEA – 17

Summary

Gain of 3 yards on the carry by Lynch

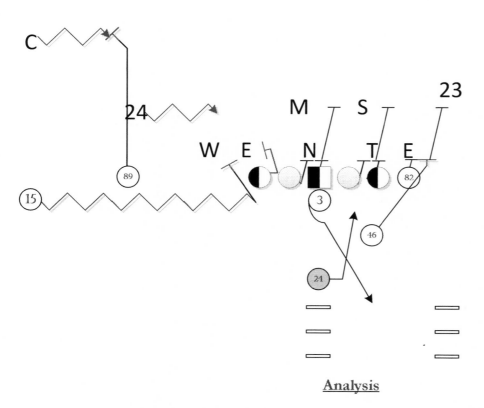

Analysis

The Sam linebacker Hightower is "plussed" to the strong side because of the fullback's offset alignment to that side.

Wilson calls in Kearse in short motion in order to cut off the pursuit of the Will linebacker up on the line of scrimmage, then opens up to the right to hand off the football to Lynch.

The front side combo between the tight end Luke Wilson and the fullback Will Tukuafu, or rather the defeat of the block front side by Rob Ninkovich is a huge part of the play Ninkovich beats Wilson right off the snap and then takes on the fullback's inside shoulder, forcing the ball outside to Hightower coming over the top of the block and Patrick Chung on the outside. Lynch picks up 3 yards after the play gets forced outside for the 1st down.

Seattle Drive 7 / Play 3 / 1ˢᵗ & 10 / +38 Yard Line / Right Hash / 7:08 3Q

NE – 14 SEA – 17

Summary

Russell Wilson picks up 20 yards and a first down on a scramble.

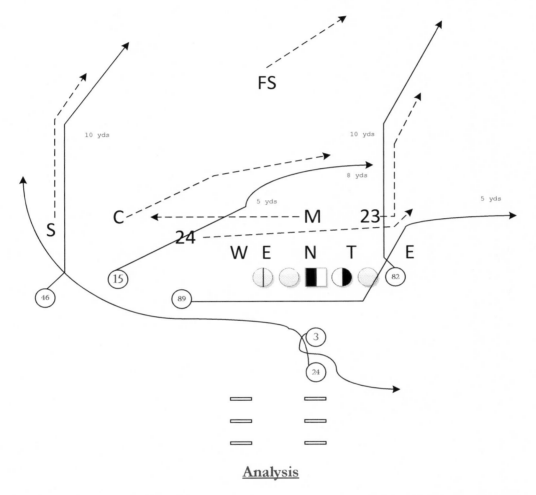

Analysis

One of the biggest questions Darrelle Bevell had to answer which preparing for this game was how would Darrelle Revis play against Doug Baldwin and how would he find creative ways to get him the football even if he goes, which has turned out to be the case tonight. One of the things Seattle does will is moving their offensive skill guys around in different areas of the formation and this comes in handy when you're trying to get the ball to your playmakers and the defense has a guy like Revis assigned to shut them down.

Baldwin runs the flat route coming underneath the offensive line as Wilson opens up to fake the wide zone to the left. As he comes around full circle, out of the fake, his eyes go to the flat/corner/drag triangle concept on the boot. The read is pretty cloudy, and Patrick Chung especially his outside leverage on Luke Wilson and the corner route he's running/

Baldwin's flat route has to avoid an unblocked Rob Ninkovich slow-playing away from the boot, and runs inside of him and immediately runs up the field to a depth of about five yards. Since the front side of the play is covered so well, Wilson looks to Lynch running the wheel route to the other side of the field, is flushed out of the pocket and picks up a 1st down.

Seattle Drive 7 / Play 4 / 1st & 10 / +18 Yard Line / Left Hash / 6:28 3Q

NE – 14 SEA – 17

Summary

Gain of 14 yards and a first down by Marshawn Lynch on the carry on the left side.

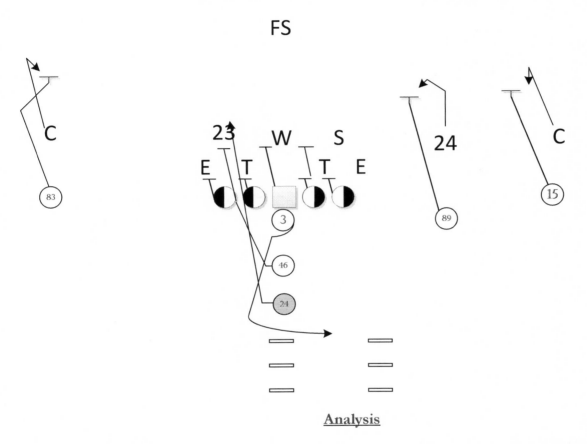

Analysis

Seattle has found a matchup they like, where the fullback fits up on the strong safety Patrick Chung on this play.

Because the offense is running to the weak side, in theory the back should be able to walk untouched into the end zone if everyone does their job. Even the FS McCourty may not be a factor depending on which way Lynch cuts up in the hole.

The idea is that the fullback should get his head outside of Chung to spring him free in the alley.

By design, the backside linebacker Jamie Collins chases down the play, along with the free safety McCourty, and gets hands on Lynch without bringing him down, and finally Ninkovich comes and runs him down from behind.

Seattle Drive 7 / Play 5 / 1ˢᵗ & Goal / +4 Yard Line / Left Hash / 5:51 3Q

NE – 14 SEA – 17

Summary

Gain of 1 yard by Lynch on the carry to the left side.

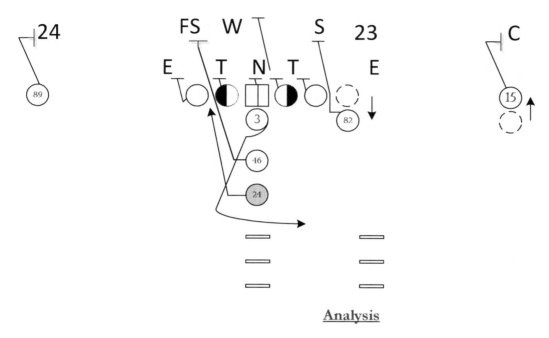

Analysis

Seattle continues to test the left side of the defense as they get closer to the goal line. Due to the alignment of the defense the play is doomed to fail from the start, since they're a man short to the weak side of the formation.

The Will linebacker Jamie Collins is unblocked as the center comes to the next level. He's got two linebackers in his face, both Collins and Hightower, the Will and the Sam, and in this case he decides to take the Sam linebacker, giving Collins an easy path to Lynch.

One interesting thing about this play is that the Seahawks move Luke Wilson off the line of scrimmage as if he's going to go in motion across the formation, but Russell Wilson decides not to bring him across in motion, so he ends up working in conjunction with the backside tackle on the play.

There's also the matter of the nose tackles working against the RG and the center. The RG does a poor job of trying to cut the nose, and as he sheds the cut block attempt, the nose Sealver Siliga, along with Collins gets his hands on Lynch and keeps him to a 1-yard gain.

Seattle Drive 7 / Play 6 / 2nd & 3 / +3 Yard Line / Middle / 5:20 3Q

NE – 14 SEA – 17

Summary

Touchdown! Pass complete to Doug Baldwin for a gain of three yards and a score.

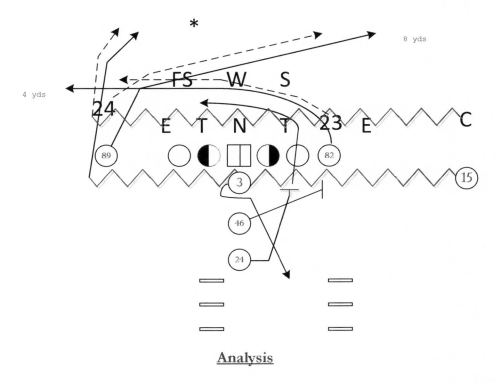

Analysis

Darrell Bevell reaches into his bag of tricks once again and finds a play specifically designed to get Doug Baldwin the football with such tight coverage inside the five yard line.

It's a matter of maximizing opportunities for one of your best players, even when the individual matchup may not work too much in your favor. For example, putting Baldwin split out wide, where he's working one-on-one against one of the best corners in the league, is not an efficient use of his abilities, at least not if you're trying to get him the football. He has to be able to win his individual matchup on the edge, not to mention that the ball is in the air for an extended period of time, meaning that the defense has a better chance at making a play on the football.

This particular play is a version of the "mesh" concept, where in this case the tight end helps rub on Revis who is trailing Baldwin across the field on the crossing route.

You'll also notice the asterisk in the diagram, just above the FS. That is the umpire, who because of Baldwin's smart route-running, plays a much bigger role in the play than he should have.

Baldwin takes the "mesh" idea to another level when he runs his route in such a way that Revis, while trailing behind him in coverage, ends up colliding with the umpires as he's coming across the field.

Wilson brings Kearse in motion from right to left and settles up behind Baldwin before the snap, Wilson takes the snap, opens up 180 degrees to his left to fake to Lynch. He'll peek for just a second at Kearse on the bend route, but as he sees Baldwin start to come open once he gets past the midpoint of the field, he lets the football go. Baldwin has to make a diving catch but Seattle extends their lead in the game.

Seattle PAT / New England PAT Block

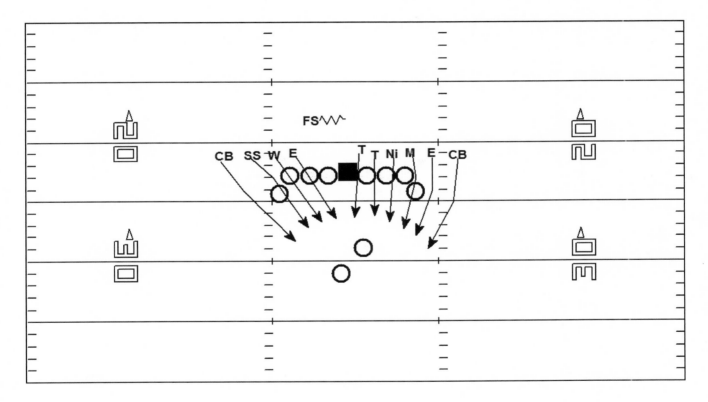

Seattle Drive #7 Review

With New England suddenly starting to cover up all three interior linemen, Seattle decides to attack just off-tackle and try to pin the defense inside, using their tight alignments against them.

The offense goes back to the hitch play on the outside on 1st down, and the choice to pass on 1st down is a good once since it's a high-percentage throw that Wilson has already completed in this game, and it's to the single-receiver side off of play action.

When the offense gets down to the goal line, it's clear they've got the assignments down of the ILB's since they go right after Hightower with the fake to the strong side, while along with the rub from Baldwin on the umpire as he's crossing the field, creates a wide open passing lane for the score.

For Belichick, there's not much he can draw up for his defense on the sideline at this point. New England is getting guys to the football, but they're just not wrapping up and making the tackle on Lynch. Just another example of why the mantra "Do your job" is so important for the Patriots. It really is that simple.

Seattle Kickoff

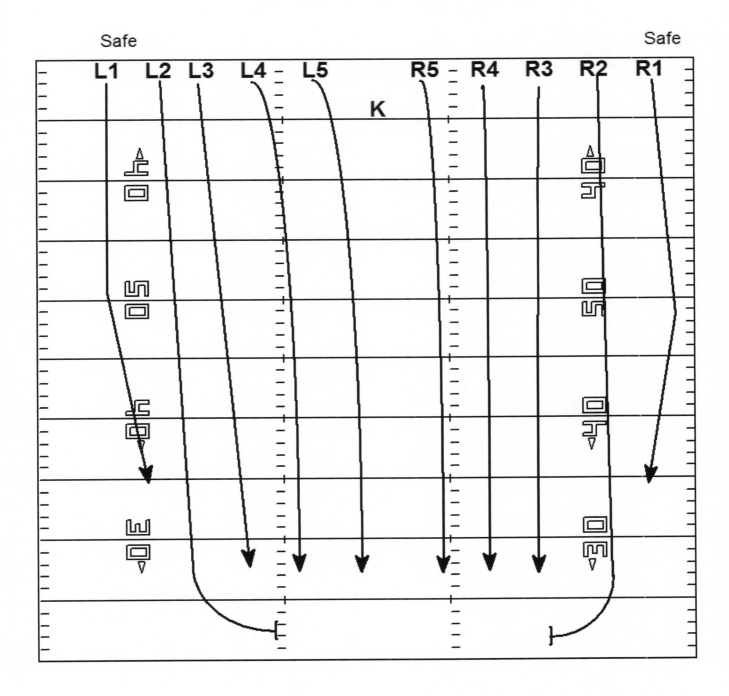

New England Kickoff Return

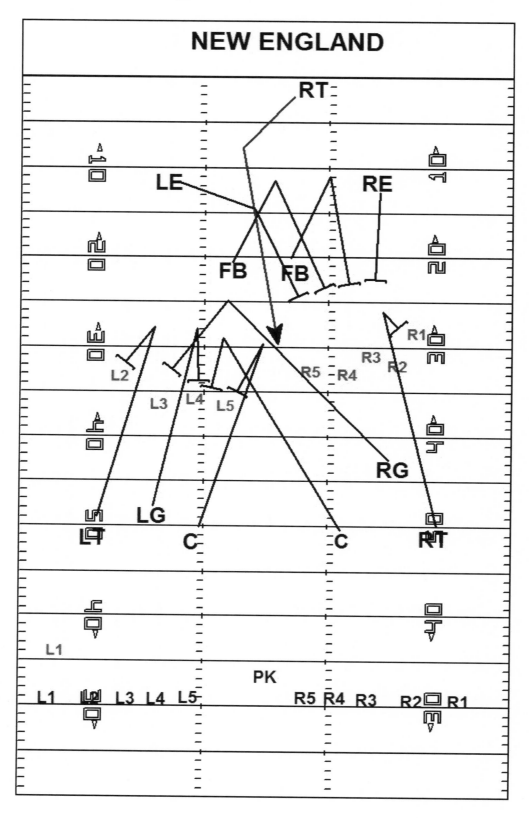

New England Drive 7 / Play 1 / 1ˢᵗ & 10 / -35 Yard Line / Left Hash / 4:48 3Q

NE – 14 SEA – 24

Summary

Pass complete to Edelman on the deep left side for a gain of 18 yards, but a holding penalty negates the play and brings the ball back 10 yards.

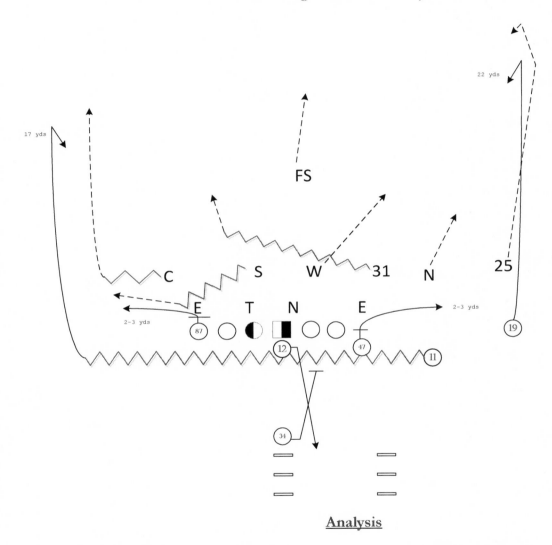

Analysis

There's a pretty simple idea on this play: "Go run to a spot and I'll throw it to you." The pair of deep comeback routes at different depths are timed up to come open at different intervals. If Edelman had been covered, Brandon LaFell would be coming out of the top of his route, just like that. Brady keeps his eyes locked on Earl Thomas to hold him in the middle of the field so that he can't help to either side, but Brady knows exactly where he's going with the football unless Thomas completely commits to the left side, then it becomes a one-on-one battle with Sherman.

The important part of the play design is that the route breaks past the point of underneath defenders where they can't undercut the route.

New England Drive 7 / Play 2 / 1ˢᵗ & 20 / -25 Yard Line / Left Hash / 4:37 3Q

NE – 14 SEA – 24

Summary

Deep pass intended for Brandon LaFell incomplete along the deep left sideline.

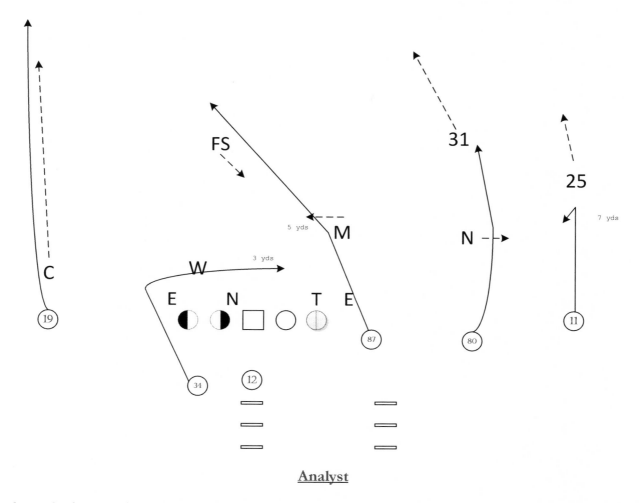

Analyst

Brady reads the two-deep shell and watches Earl Thomas rotates down low and Chancellor is the single-high safety all the way to the right hash, leaving LaFell one-on-one down the left sideline.

The only problem is that the split is so close to the sideline that LaFell has almost no room to operate when the ball is in the air to go get it.

The offense is picking on the nickel Tharold Simon who is replacing Jeremy Lane after his shoulder injury in the 1st quarter, and so far he's been holding his own for the first part.

New England Drive 7 / Play 3 / 2nd & 20 / -25 Yard Line / Left Hash / 4:13 3Q

NE – 14 SEA – 24

Summary

Pass complete underneath to Edelman for a gain of 11 yards.

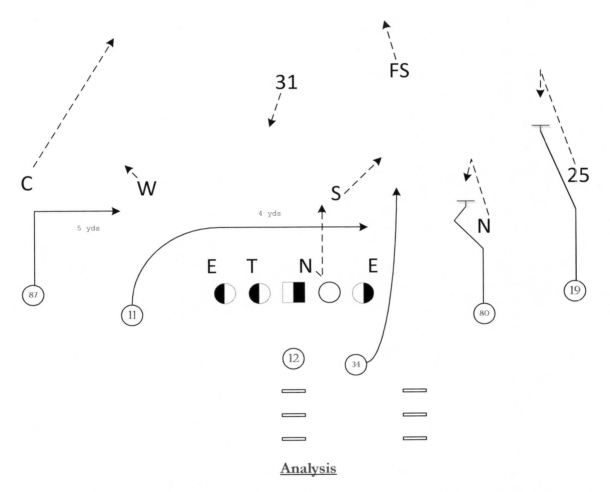

Analysis

This is a well-timed downfield screen created by the Patriots so they can create an extra way to get the football to Edelman in the middle of the field.

What normally happens away from the shallow cross route is packaged with at least one clear out route to open up the entire right side of the field and create a running lane for the guy running the shallow crossing route. In this case, it's basically like a receiver screen like many offenses run to the backside of run plays, only this time the receiver is coming from the opposite side of the formation.

This is an example of a play that an offensive coordinator keeps circled on his call sheet for when he needs a play that is practically guaranteed to pick up at least 7-8 yards. Based on the drop of the defenders to that side, and the down and distance situation, it was pretty much a lock to get back a lot of the yardage lost to the penalty from earlier.

New England Drive 7 / Play 4 / 3rd & 9 / -36 Yard Line / Right Hash / 3:53 3Q

NE – 14 SEA – 24

Summary

Pass incomplete intended for Amendola underneath to the left side.

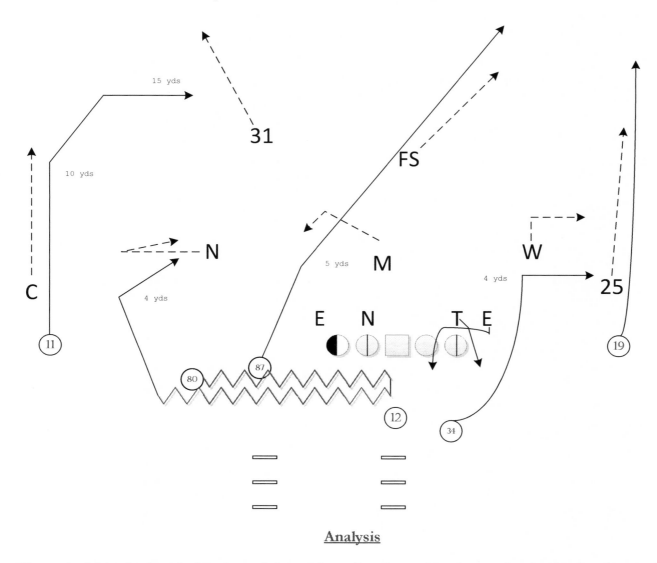

Analysis

The goal of this play is to isolate Amendola on Maxwell underneath so he can do what he does best and get the yards after the catch and pick up the first down.

Gronkowski's route up the middle of the field designed to split the safeties and hopefully hold the Mike linebacker in place as he carries the vertical route deep which will open up the middle of the field underneath. If for some reason Amendola can't get any leverage on his defender, Brady has two options.

He can either upset reset his feet and look for Vereen breaking to the flat on the opposite side, or more likely he'll wait for Edelman to come open on the dig route at about 15 yards, and developing behind the pivot route behind Amendola.

New England Punt

PRO PUNT 46 BASE

2   3   4   5 5   4   3   2   1

1

Seattle Punt Return

46 BASE   4 HOLD RET MID

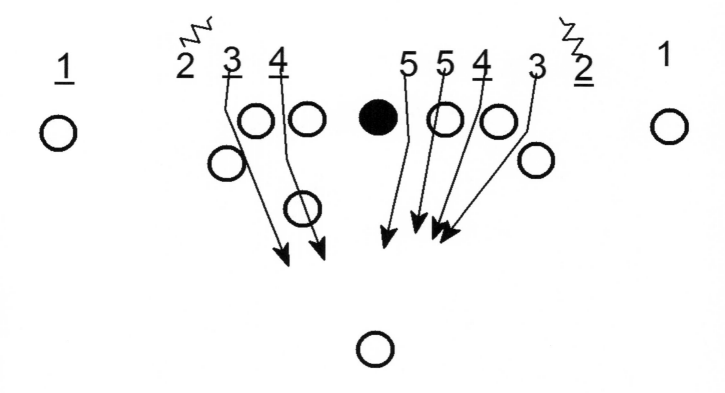

New England Drive #7 Review

A promising drive is cut short by an offensive penalty that puts New England in a hole on 1st and 20.

One notable adjustment by New England's offense on play #3 is that they manage to find another way to get the football to Edelman on the shallow cross route, this time out of a 2x2 formation when the Seahawk defense is not expecting it.

At this point, New England has all but given up on the run game, and since they don't have a reliable way to gain four yards on first down as opposed to putting the offense in a position where they have to take shots down the field in order to get any consistent movement.

Seattle Drive 8 / Play 1 / 1ˢᵗ & 10 / -20 Yard Line / Middle / 3:15 3Q

NE – 14 SEA – 24

Summary

Pass complete to Ricardo Lockette down the deep middle of the field for a gain of 25 yards and a first down.

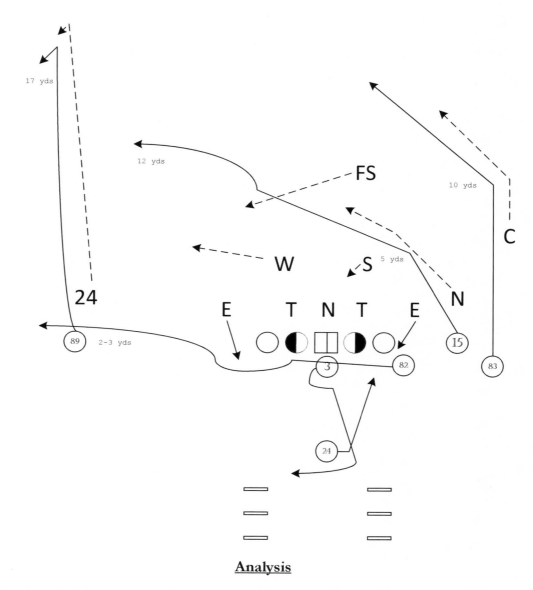

Analysis

Seattle has New England on their heels at this point, and the Seahawks are going in for the kill.

Seattle lines up in a bunch formation that they've used a couple of times already tonight to run the inside zone play. Now they've set themselves up nicely for the play action pass down the field out of this formation, and as a complement to the run scheme.

As Wilson comes out of his play fake, he immediately looks for their backside post ran by Lockette as McCourty comes downhill into the weak side alley and leaves the deep middle of the field completely wide open. Wilson waits at least a second too long to get the football. If he could've thrown the football a little quicker as Lockette is beginning to make his break into the middle of the field, this is probably a touchdown, or at the very least would give him room to run underneath the throw and catch it in stride for a bigger gain.

Seattle Drive 8 / Play 2 / 1ˢᵗ & 10 / -45 / Left Hash / 2:52 3Q

NE – 14 SEA – 24

Summary

Gain of 2 yards on the carry by Marshawn Lynch up the middle.

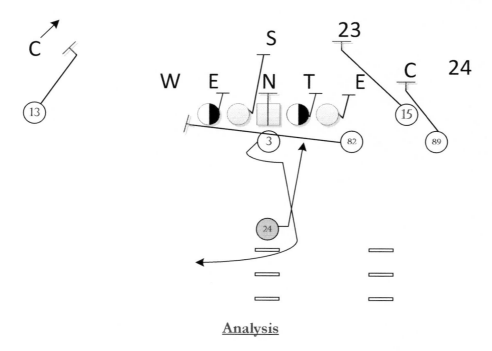

Analysis

Staying in the same formation and personnel group, this time Seattle hands the football up the middle on the wham play that they've run a couple of times already.

Trouble occurs on this play as Chandler Jones, originally lined up on the inside shoulder of the left tackle, ends up beating his block at the line of scrimmage.

After giving the tackle a quick stutter move to the inside, forcing the left tackle to move too far to the inside to protect the B gap, Jones then uses the left tackle's weight against him, using a swim move to beat him to the outside and taking advantage of an offensive lineman whose weight is now focused too far to his inside. Jones gets past the blockers in front of him, shoots into the backfield and helps hold Lynch to a 2 yard gain.

Seattle Drive 8 / Play 3 / 2ⁿᵈ & 8 / -47 Yard Line / Right Hash / 2:05 3Q

NE – 14 SEA – 24

Summary

Pass complete to Jermain Kearse on the hitch route on the right side for a gain of 4 yards.

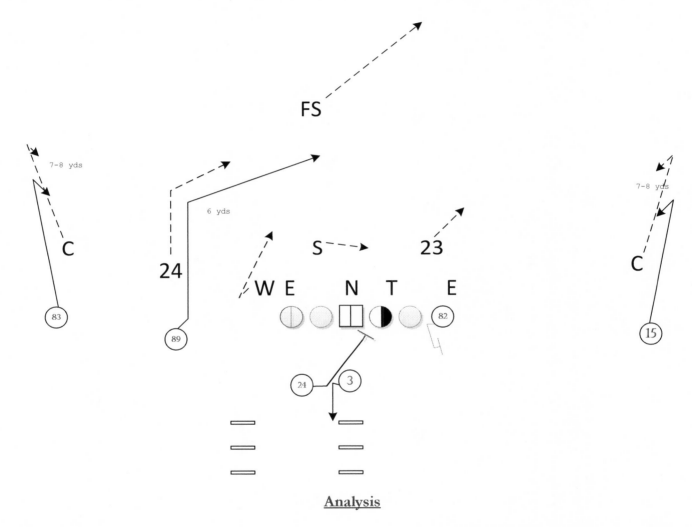

Analysis

Kearse cuts his route for some reason on this play, and ends up setting up 3rd and short. It's a combination of Wilson having to put the ball behind him because of the tight coverage of Malcolm Butler, but also because it's just a route that's run short to begin with.

The tight man coverage the Patriots have been playing all game lends itself to routes like these, where it comes down to guys like Kearse winning their individual matchups and using their natural size advantage to win at the line of scrimmage and when the ball is in the air.

Seattle Drive 8 / Play 4 / 3ʳᵈ & 3 / +48 Yard Line / Right Hash / 1:30 3Q

NE – 14 SEA – 24

Summary

Pass intended for Jermain Kearse deep down the left sideline is incomplete.

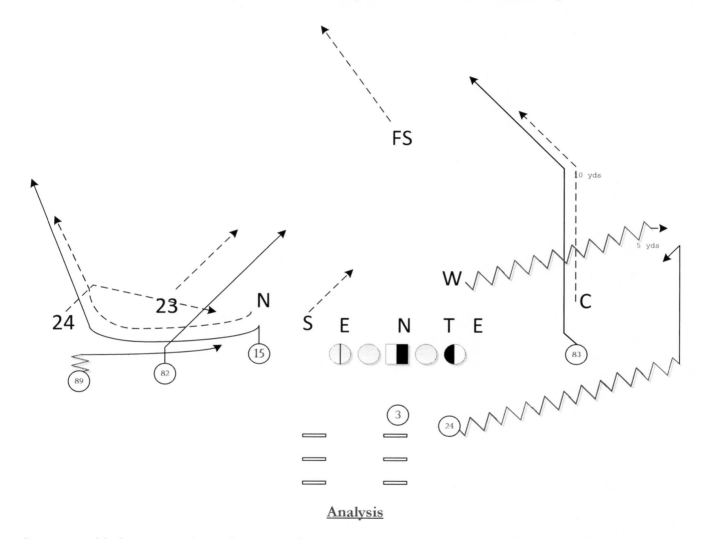

Analysis

On paper, this is a great play call. It's another very creative way to get the football to one of their best receivers, but on 3rd and 3 in New England territory, this kind of play isn't necessary, especially with the kind of success Seattle has had running the football out of the gun.

The basis of the play is that the Seattle offense is faking a receiver screen out wide to the left to Baldwin, and #15 Jermaine Kearse starts on a path as if he's going to block out on the corner (Revis) to get up an alley and seal off the outside to make room for Baldwin.

Luke Wilson the tight end runs a 2-step slant that's really set up to create a rub on the defensive back over Kearse as he's running his extended wheel route. Baldwin runs his normal route, staying on the same kind of path he would've run if it was a true receiver screen, and runs inside as the 3rd option on the play. Kearse actually almost makes the play on the sideline, but he can't quite hold on to the pass.

The New England defense is slow-playing the pass rush, making sure to muddy-up the running lanes up the middle and keep Wilson in the pocket. They also drop the Sam linebacker and the right defensive end into the shallow zones underneath to protect against the short passes, but it's tight coverage from Malcolm Butler that forces Seattle to bring on the punt team.

Seattle Punt

PRO PUNT55 BASE

2   3   4   5   5   4   3   2   1

1

New England Punt Return

55 BASE   8 MAN BLOCK

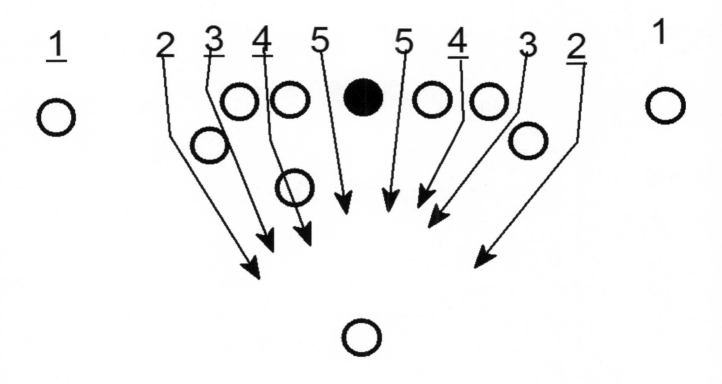

Seattle Drive #8 Review

Seattle finds another way to attack the bear front being run by New England on the 1st play, and they force the Patriots to adjust their personnel on the field after hitting the deep post route over the middle on 1st down.

New England is forced to bring another safety, Patrick Chung, back onto the field to adjust to the threats, and free up the FS to play in the middle of the field as an extra pass defender.

The Patriots have begun to clamp down on the run, and more than that, have tackled much better on this drive. Perhaps most telling of all is that Seattle has begun to rely more and more on unfamiliar plays, especially on the 3rd down, where a complicated attempt to get a man free down the sideline results in a very low-percentage pass.

New England is forcing Seattle to do things they're not entirely comfortable with, and a long part of that comes from winning on 1st down. While the Patriots defense took a defensive tackle off the field after the big play on 1st down, they keep their base nickel personnel and keep them aligned in a similar look, covering up the interior linemen, with Hightower playing the weak side edge, and Collins assigned as the ILB who the defensive linemen up front are assigned to keep unblocked.

Drive 8 / Play 1 / 1st & 10 / -14 Yard Line / Right Hash / 0:55 3Q

NE – 14 SEA – 24

Summary

Gain of three yards on the run up the middle by Vereen.

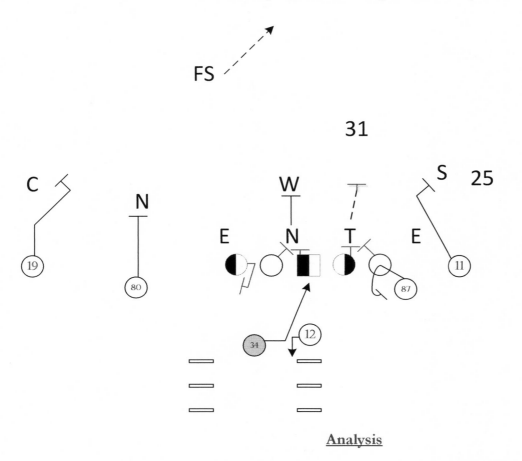

Analysis

The clock is starting to become a factor with just over a quarter left in regulation and New England down 10 points.

The Patriots line up in the same formation they've used earlier in the game to package a slant/flat concept with a power fake, this time it's more of a draw play up the middle with Vereen.

It's worth mentioning that with all the trouble New England has had running the football against this Seattle defense, they're now trying to use Vereen instead of Blount as the runner, in an attempt to throw of Seattle's defense.

Traditionally over the last few games, Blount has been the go-to back for moving the football on the ground, but now grasping for anything, they're handing it off up the middle to Vereen.

New England Drive 8 / Play 2 / 2nd & 7 / -17 Yard Line / Right Hash / 0:40 3Q

NE – 14 SEA – 24

Summary

Pass complete to Develin in the left flat for a gain of 6 yards.

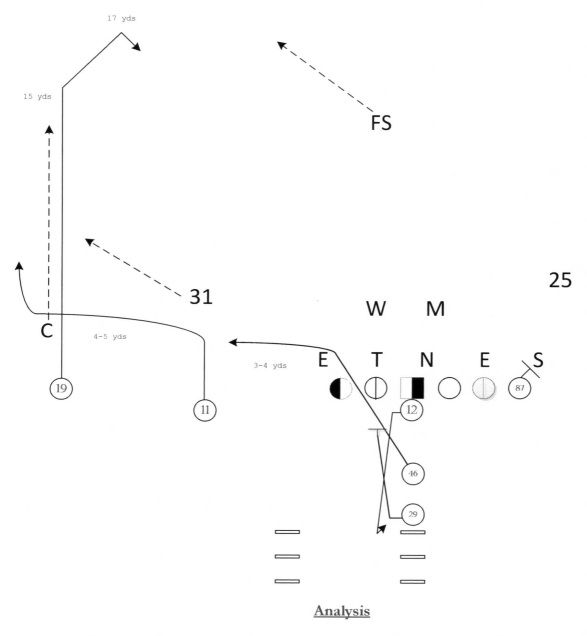

Analysis

New England has found a way to create some space out of the twins formation, by running the X receiver deep on a curl route, then having the Z receiver widen out on the wheel route, and all of a sudden the fullback Develin is wide open in the flat with no one around him. If he was any faster, he picks up the first down, but he's got the speed of a typical fullback and sets up another third and short.

New England Drive 8 / Play 3 / 3rd & 1 / -23 Yard Line / Left Hash / 15:00 4Q

NE – 14 SEA – 24

Summary

Blount is stopped in the backfield for a loss of 2 yards on the run to the right.

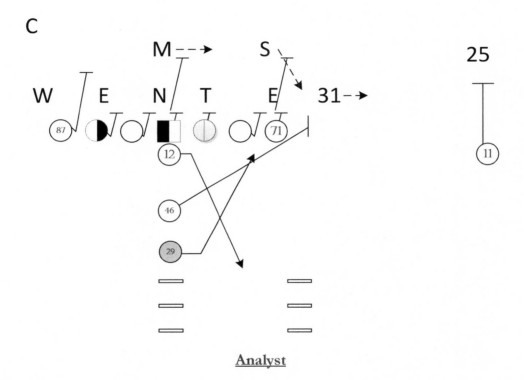

Analyst

New England looks for one yard out of this formation, but can't pick it up and once again the wide zone play is stuffed in the backfield. The Patriots haven't even tried to show any other offensive look from this formation.

The front side combo on this play between the tight end and right tackle, or rather the lack of a combo, is what really dooms this play. The Sam linebacker to the front side of the play comes over the top of the potential combo by the tight end and cuts off the running lane for Blount.

New England Punt

PRO PUNT 55 SAFE

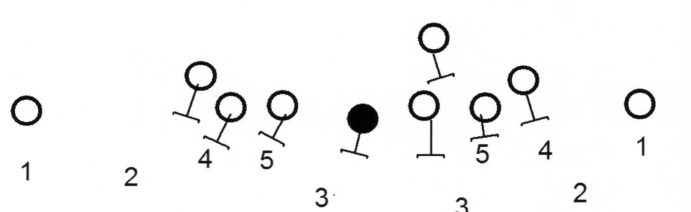

Seattle Punt Return

55 SAFE   SAFE RET

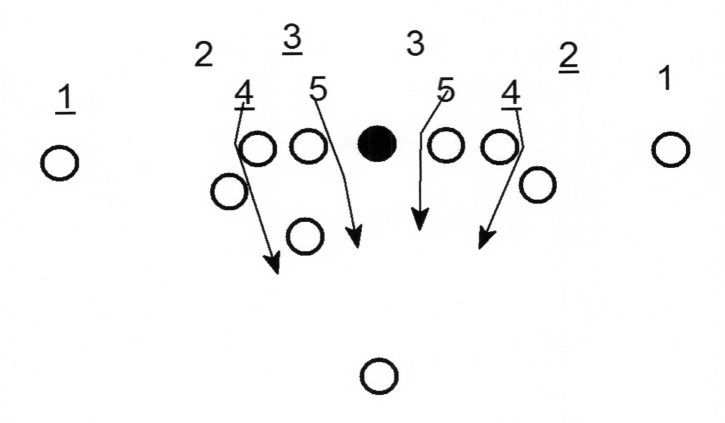

New England Drive #8 Review

It's clear that Seattle has made adjustments in their short yardage defense, and New England needs another answer is the run game in order to keep some semblance of balance.

At this point Dan Quinn has told his guys to not even worry about Gronkowski's side of the tight formation out of 22 personnel. Earlier in the drive on 1st down, the Patriots attempted to get the football to Shane Vereen out of the gun in the run game. Then on 3rd and short, the offense can't even get a big enough push to pick up a single yard, and New England has to go back to the drawing board.

Seattle Drive 9 / Play 1 / 1ˢᵗ & 10 / -36 Yard Line / Right Hash / 14:17 4Q

NE – 14 SEA – 24

Summary

Gain of 2 yards on the carry to the left side by Marshawn Lynch.

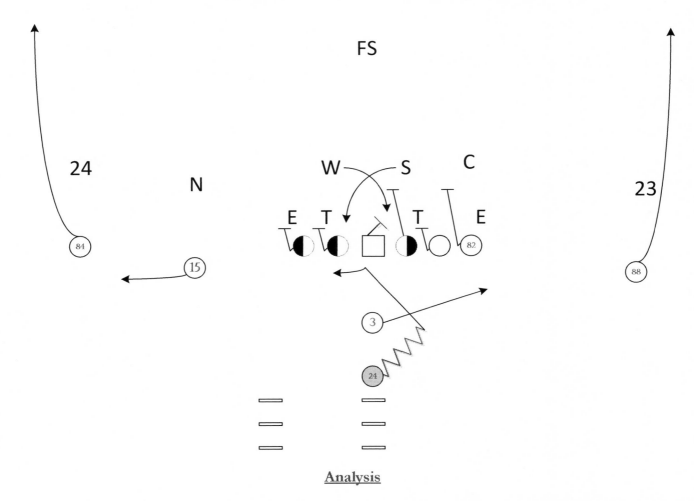

Analysis

On the 1st play of this drive Seattle continues to make offensive adjustments, and anticipates the kind of defensive front that they'll be getting against this personnel group and formation.

The Seahawks bring out their 12 personnel on 1st down, expecting a loaded tackle box with 7 men, including Patrick Chung at the strong safety position, aligned over the tight end.

By putting the 2nd tight end out at the Z receiver spot out wide to the right, they effectively remove a great run defender from the box by forcing him to cover a guy in a position who wouldn't be involved in the play anyway.

New England brings a specific kind of cross-blitz to stop the run game up the middle since they're counting on Russell Wilson not to take off with the ball. The Will linebacker stunts into the opposite A gap to occupy the center while the Sam comes in behind as the 2nd blitzer into the unoccupied gap.

As the Sam shows up in the A gap, he forces Lynch out wider to the DT Alan Branch and Lynch still manages to pick up 2 yards.

Seattle Drive 9 / Play 2 / 2nd & 8 / -38 Yard Line / Left Hash / 13:55 4Q

NE – 14 SEA – 24

Summary

Gain of 1 yard by Lynch on the carry up the middle.

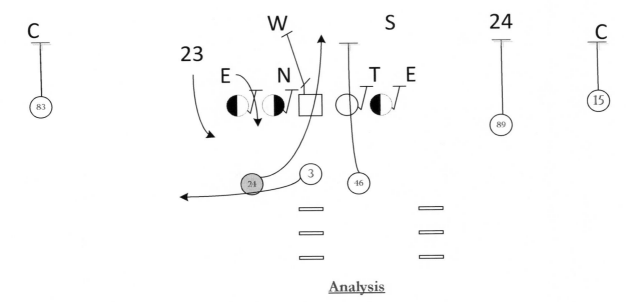

Analysis

Seattle brings the fullback back on the field, now getting into a more conservative mode, since they've been limited somewhat by Wilson's inaccuracy and the excellent defense by New England.

The Patriots come off the edge on the weak side blitz with Patrick Chung because of the down and distance situation and the personnel on the field.

It's the first time they've tried to run this play in the game out of the 2-back gun, and it has some potential.

Unfortunately for Seattle this play hinges on the right guard's ability to block Vince Wilfork one-on-one, an assignment he's struggled with all game long. Wilfork shoots through the gap and helps bring down Lynch after a gain of a yard.

Seattle Drive 9 / Play 3 / 3rd & 7 / -39 Yard Line / Middle / 13:17 4Q

NE – 14 SEA – 24

Summary

Sack! Russell Wilson is taken down by Rob Ninkovich who comes stunting from his original position as a strong defensive end position and a loss of 9 yards.

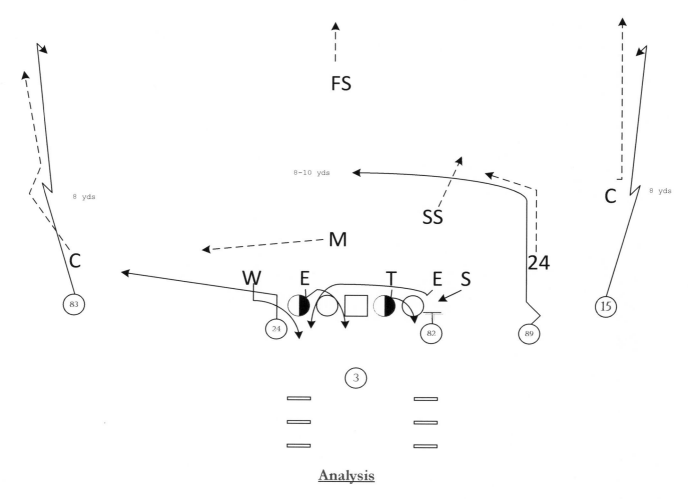

Analysis

Seattle goes back to a concept they've come to rely on in this game and this time they use a complementary play to take advantage of a defensive backfield that may try to be aggressive and jump the routes that have been run all game long.

They line up in a peculiar empty formation that they haven't run before in the game. Whereas usually in this concept Lynch is aligned in the backfield and taking part in the play action concepts and fake, and now he's aligned pre-snap off the hip of the left tackle running a flat route to the left.

Lynch is running an outlet route that would not be a good idea to run if the play was the standard expanding hitch route that the Seahawks have been running for much of the game. The main reason is that offensive coordinators don't like to run a route underneath the hitch route for fear attracting flat defenders to undercut the hitch route as they widen to cover any underneath routes from the slot or the backfield.

Rob Ninkovich brings this drive to an end as part of the 5-man pressure that New England brings on this play Ninkovich starts out wide outside the right tackle, then comes all the way around to the opposite side of the offensive line into the B gap almost completely untouched and brings down Wilson before he can get rid of the football.

Seattle Punt

PRO PUNT 54 STACK

3 4 5 5 4 3 2 1

1

2

New England Punt Return

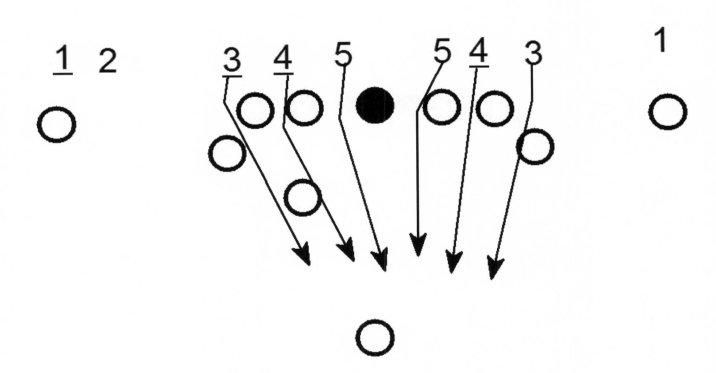

54 SAFE   4 HOLD RET MID

Seattle Drive #9 Review

Seattle is quickly running out of answer on offense, and they go back to the 13 personnel on 1st down to run the ball out of the gun, but the Patriots have been keyed in on the personnel groups on 1st and 2nd down, which puts Seattle in 3rd and long.

The hitch-and-go on 3rd down is a great constraint call for the hitch play that the offense is running several times during the 2nd half, but it puts Russell Wilson in a tough spot to have to hit a deep pass down either sideline, but he's taken down in the backfield before he can get rid of the football.

New England Drive 9 / Play 1 / 1ˢᵗ & 10 / -32 Yard Line / Right Hash / 12:10 4Q

NE – 14 SEA – 24

Summary

Sack! Tom Brady is tackled in the backfield by #51 Bruce Irvin, who lined up at defensive end opposite the left tackle.

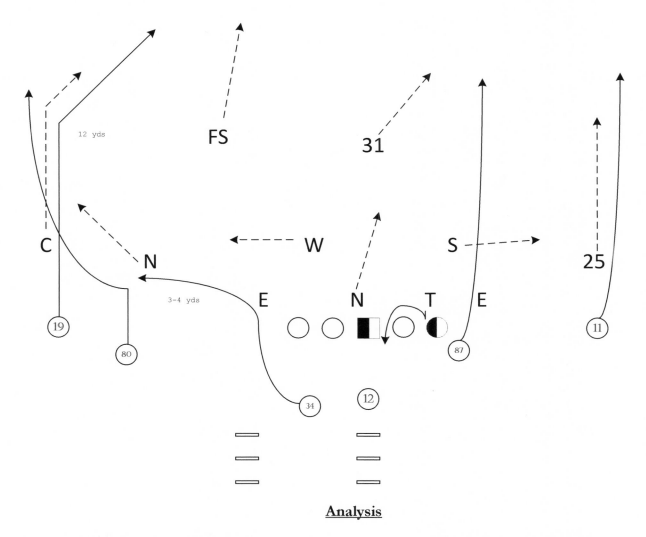

Analysis

Brady is waiting on LaFell to come open deep over the middle on the post route. He had several opportunities to get the football to Amendola on the wheel route or in the flat to Vereen once he makes a cut to the outside, but he waits too long and gets taken down in the backfield and sets the offense back 8 yards on 1st down.

To the opposite side of the play, the wide split by Edelman is designed to create space for Gronkowski down the seam, especially in case Seattle rotates to a single-safety look like they have shown a pattern of doing lately.

The sack puts a lot of pressure on the Patriots to get back on schedule and make some positive yardage to set up a manageable 3rd down situation.

New England Drive 9 / Play 2 / 2ⁿᵈ & 18 / -24 Yard Line / Middle / 11:50 4Q

NE – 14 SEA – 24

Summary

Pass complete to Brandon LaFell on the receiver screen to the right flat for a gain of 4 yards.

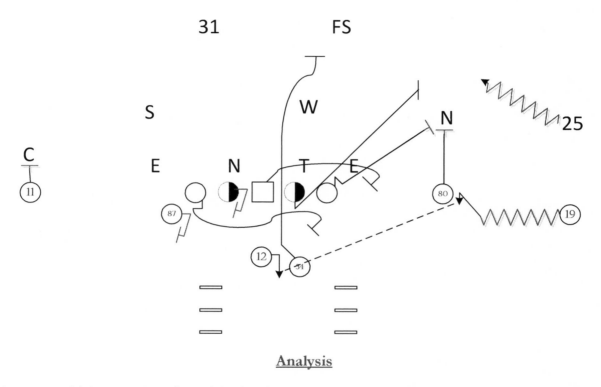

Analysis

This is a pretty high-percentage/low-risk play that's almost guaranteed to pick up a few yards. Because of the amount of shallow crossing routes and post-wheel plays from the stacked receiver look, the corner over LaFell (Sherman) is supposed to gain depth as the two receivers come closer together.

Most teams that use receiver screens don't release their tackles out to the edge, but the positive side of doing this is that you get the blockers out on the edge right away and can create a secure alley for the ball carrier.

Brady fakes to Vereen then gets the ball out on the edge to LaFell. Meanwhile, Vereen continues his path down the field and gets into the secondary to get a body on the safety.

I love the design of the play, because the center and left tackle are assigned to peel back and protect the backside of the play and remove the threat of defensive players chasing the play from behind.

After catching the pass, LaFell immediately gets up the field and is pushed out of bounds after a gain of 4 yards. The emphasis is on getting yardage now, not dancing around and looking for the right fit inside of the blocking scheme. If an obvious opportunity presents itself inside of Amendola's block, then he should take it, but usually he just needs to get north and south and get what yards he can in order to set up 3rd and manageable.

New England Drive 9 / Play 3 / 3rd & 14 / -28 Yard Line / Right Hash / 11:20 4Q

NE – 14 SEA – 24

Summary

Pass complete to Edelman in the deep left half of the field for a gain of 19 yards and a first down.

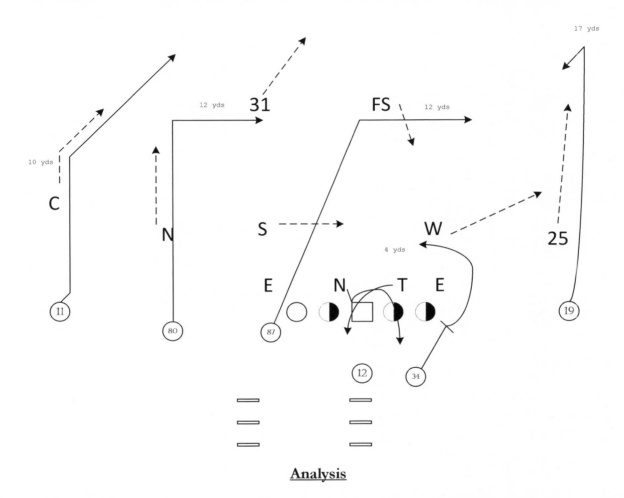

Analysis

"In clutch situations, think of players not plays." That has been one of Bill Belichick's most consistent maxims during the run of success the Patriots have enjoyed this century. This play is a perfect example of that philosophy put into action, as well as the chemistry and almost telepathic connection shared between Brady and Edelman.

By all accounts, the Seahawks do a decent job of covering the route, a post breaking in at 10 yards that is designed to come open over the dig route by Amendola clears the hash mark. The pass by Brady is a split-second later than idea, which results in a big collision in the middle of the field with Chancellor as the pass arrives, but he makes the catch and picks up the 1st down.

Commentators often joke that "there's no play in the playbook for this situation" usually talking about a long yardage 3rd down, but in this case, the Patriots have designed this play for this specific scenario.

You've got two crossing route by Gronk and Amendola breaking in at just underneath the 1st down marker, and slowly fading to gain depth past the chains as they cross the field. LaFell also contributes by lining up so wide and getting deep enough on the comeback route at 17 yards and still create a window in the coverage for the crosser coming in behind him.

Then you have Edelman, breaking across the face of the corner running over the top of him and finding the tiniest of creases between that defender and the FS. It's great players executing a smart play design at a high level, and the drive continues with a fresh set of downs.

New England Drive 9 / Play 4 / 1ˢᵗ & 10 / -49 Yard Line / Left Hash / 10:25 4Q

NE – 14 SEA – 24

Summary

Pass complete to Vereen on the tailback screen to the left for a gain of nine yards. (Unnecessary roughness penalty called on Seattle after the play for an extra 15 yards and a first down)

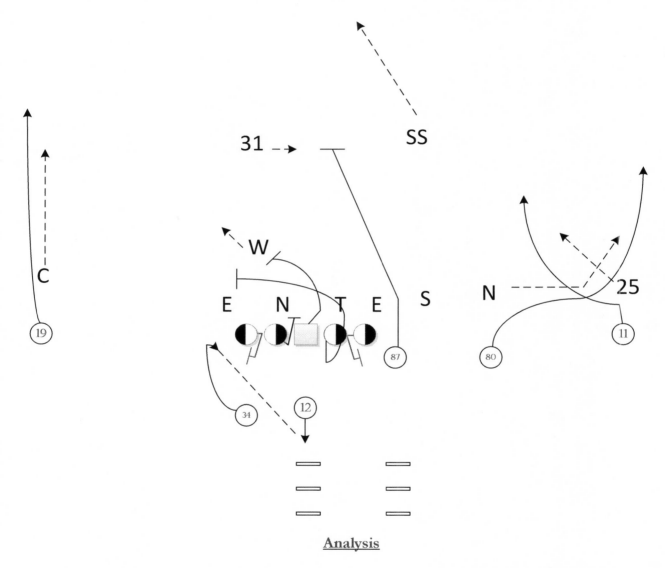

Analysis

Just recently running a receiver screen a couple of plays before, the time seems right to give Seattle a similar look to the 3 receiver side and end up sending the football back in the other direction.

Brady drops back and eyes the crossing receiver routes by Edelman and Amendola to the right. This doesn't have much of an influence on the men on the field for Seattle, since they're each locked up on the guy across from them in man coverage, but it does help Brady time up his drop and know when to get Vereen the football as he sets up outside the left tackle.

Since New England lines up in a 3x1 set and is getting the ball to the alley on the single receiver side of the formation, there aren't a lot of defenders to that side other than the Will lined up across from Vereen, so as a result there isn't a need for as many offensive linemen, which is why you only see two linemen release to the weak side. The center does a great job of blocking two people by engaging the Will backer out in space and getting in the way of Chancellor who comes hard downhill once the ball gets to Vereen.

Seattle gives New England a 1st down after hitting Vereen out of bounds, and suddenly the Patriots have picked up two consecutive 1st downs on this drive, and they're well into Seattle territory.

New England Drive 9 / Play 5 / 1ˢᵗ & 10 / +27 Yard Line / Left Hash / 9:43 4Q

NE – 14 SEA – 24

Summary

Pass incomplete intended for Brandon LaFell deep left in the end zone.

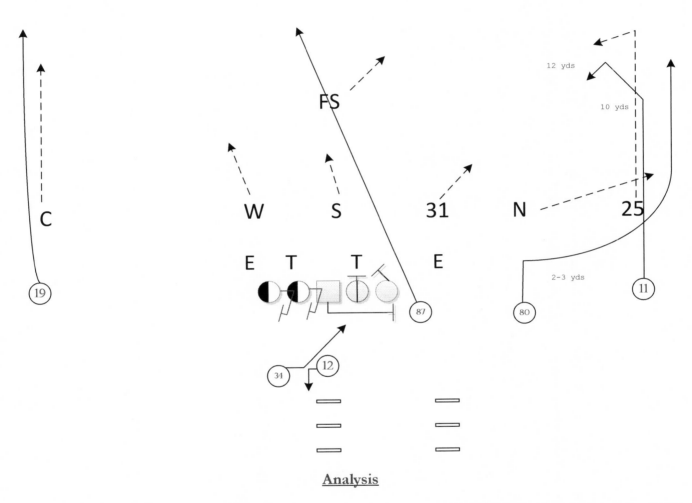

Analysis

Now within field goal range, the Patriots decide to go deep again on this drive thanks to some play action with a pulling lineman.

The decision to target LaFell instead of Gronkowski on this play was made before the snap when Earl Thomas had his heels inside the left hash and Tavon Wilson was lined up one-on-one across from LaFell, and it was confirmed when Thomas stepped even further away from the single receiver side after the snap and during the course of the play fake.

Unfortunately for New England, Brady doesn't put the ball in a spot where it avoids the DB, and Wilson slaps it away at the last second before LaFell can haul it in for a quick score.

Seattle's defense is playing Thomas toward the 3 receiver side of the formation, specifically to take away any vertical route by Gronk, which is the reason why LaFell found himself matched up on the Seahawks' #3 corner one-on-one. The vertical routes by Gronk and LaFell are designed to stretch the FS to cover more ground than he's comfortable with, and that's exactly what happens here.

New England Drive 9 / Play 6 / 2nd & 10 / +27 Yard Line / Left Hash / 9:28 4Q

NE – 14 SEA – 24

Summary

Gain of 2 yards on the run by Vereen to the right side.

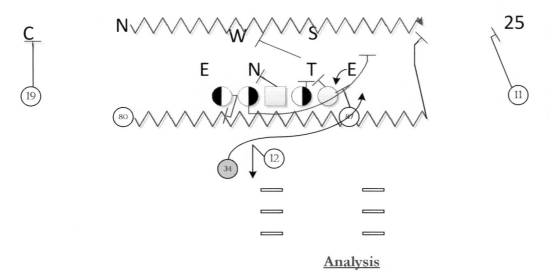

Analysis

Yet again, the Patriots face another 2nd and long after an incompletion on 1st down, and they line up in a 2x2 set, before motioning Danny Amendola from left to right and ending up in the exact same formation they lined up in on the previous play.

In this situation, the Seahawks stay in a 2-deep shell, while keeping Byron Maxwell locked in on Amendola as he moves from left to right. The Patriots want to get some positive yardage to set up a 3rd and manageable situation. They're also working on solving another problem their offensive line has had to face all game long, finding a reliable way to run the football. At this point they're using any trick they can think of, and that includes handing it off to Vereen out of the gun, as opposed to Blount who takes most of the handoffs when the offense goes under center.

The power play out of the gun is another attempt to manufacture a run game, and having Gronkowski on the field at the point of attack sitting off the right hip of the right tackle is a huge advantage when you're trying to create an edge in the run game, either running between the tackles or outside in the alley.

The pulling guard initially is looking to turn up to the 2nd level inside of Gronkowski's block, but the DE does a good job of squeezing the amount of space in the C gap, and forces the guard to pull around the outside hip. This makes it tougher for the defensive line to get to the guys at the 2nd level, since they're running to the outside and aren't where they would be normally if the play hit off-tackle.

New England Drive 9 / Play 7 / 3rd & 8 / +25 Yard Line / Right Hash / 9:10 4Q

NE – 14 SEA – 24

Summary

Pass complete to Edelman over the middle for a gain of 20 yards and a first down.

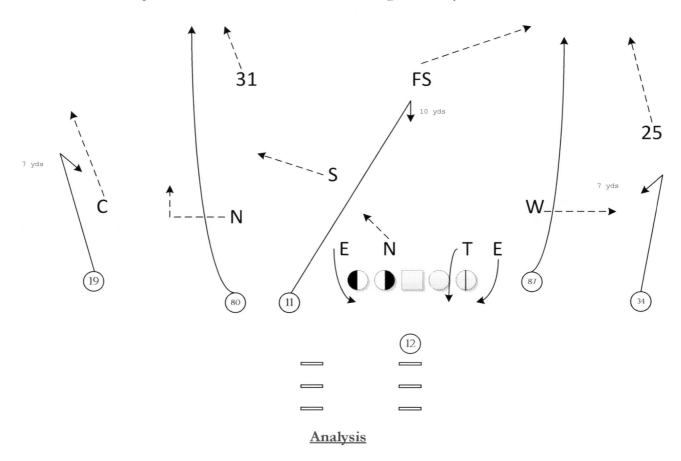

Analysis

New England lines up in an empty set on 3rd down looking to spread the defense thin, especially up the middle since Seattle is playing with a 2-deep shell. Like the previous 3rd down, this play call is all about getting the ball to your clutch player, which for Brady is Julian Edelman.

The Patriots forced the defense into declaring their intentions before the snap because of the way they've flip-flopped their personnel, and sending all three receivers to the left and Gronk and Vereen to the right.

Edelman was basically told to get in the middle, get past the chains, and get open. His path is blocked initially by the nose tackle, dropping into coverage and opening to his side, presumably to take away any shallow or slant route that Edelman had been torching Seattle with all game long. #95 Demarcus Dobbs is the nose tackle who drops into the middle for the Seahawks, and Edelman's only real job is to get past and around him so that Brady can get him the ball in that sweet spot between the safeties.

New England Drive 9 / Play 7 / 3rd & 8 / +25 Yard Line / Right Hash / 9:10 4Q

NE – 14 SEA – 24

Summary

Pass intended for Edelman in the left flat is incomplete.

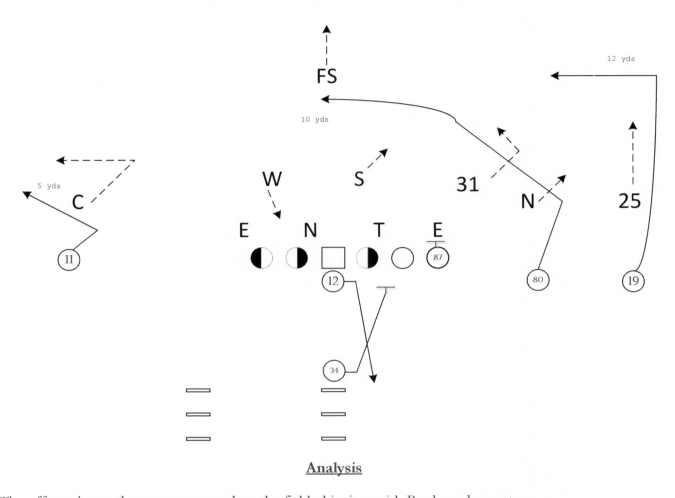

Analysis

The offense keeps the same personnel on the field, this time with Brady under center.

At the snap, Brady opens up to the right and extends the football to the midsection of Vereen and then rotates his shoulders and body to get in position for the throw to Edelman. Unfortunately, he lets the ball fly a bit too high for Edelman, who was wide open after completely shaking Tharold Simon, the corner, at the line of scrimmage.

Earl Thomas stands deep in the end zone at the FS position, and Chancellor is rotated down in the alley between Amendola and Gronk so Edelman is facing pure man-to-man coverage. This is where formation plays a huge part in the coverage New England is facing. Since Seattle is not fond of removing linebackers from the tackle box, and does not want to give Gronkowski soft coverage for the dump pass, the trips formation New England lines up in virtually assures that Edelman will be one-on-one to his side with no extra defensive help.

Thomas standing in the middle of the field is playing as an extra run defender, as well as helping on any crossing routes over the middle and kind of route off of play action for Gronk so he doesn't go over the middle uncontested.

New England Drive 9 / Play 9 / 2ⁿᵈ & Goal / +5 Yard Line / Right Hash / 8:00 4Q

NE – 14 SEA – 24

Summary

Touchdown! Pass completed to Danny Amendola in the back of the end zone for a gain of five yards and a score.

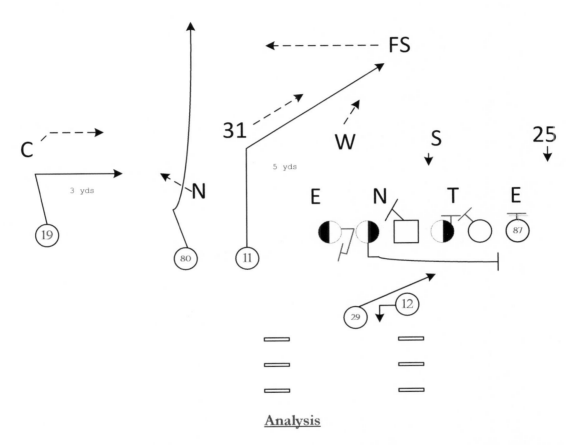

Analysis

The defense is intent on defending the actual goal line, and so the Patriots put in a play designed to stretch the coverage past the goal line.

LaFell slants out with a vertical release before cutting across the field at a 3 yard depth. The defenders have their heels on the goal line to stop the kind of quick cuts in and out against the tight man coverage that Edelman got so wide open on during the previous play. It's also because of the formation New England has lined up in which allows them to run some route concepts that switch up with one another. Add to this the Patriots' fondness for running the shallow cross concept, and it's in Seattle's best interest to put several pass defenders on the goal line to disrupt the shallow cross concept.

LaFell's route is designed to occupy the underneath defenders, or get open if he can while staying on his trajectory, while Amendola and Edelman stretch the back end of the coverage. Brady reads it from left to right, and when the corner (Maxwell) releases Amendola and passes him off to Thomas, there's enough room in the back of the end zone for Brady to get the football to Amendola.

New England PAT / Seattle PAT Block

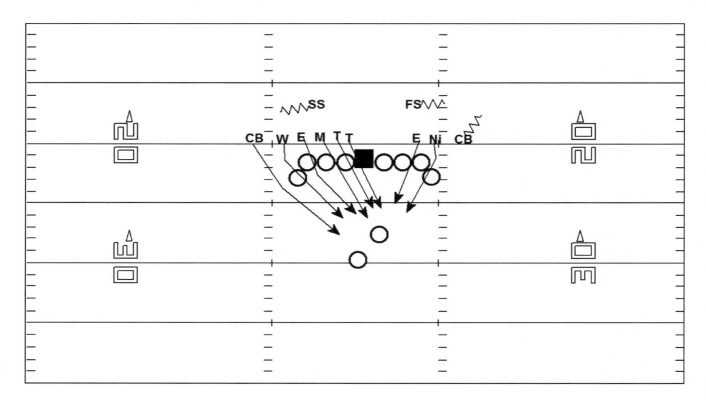

New England Drive #9 Review

This drive was nearly stopped in its tracks twice due to 3rd and long situations, but both times Julian Edelman comes up big down the field.

The Patriots still have yet to establish a consistent running game or a way to get a regular four yard gain to win on 1st down, but at the moment it doesn't seem to matter as much since they're knocking on the door down by 3 points.

Tharold Simon continues to be one of the biggest targets on the field for New England, especially when he gets isolated to the single receiver side of the trips formation down on the goal line. Even though Brady can't quite get the football to Edelman on the route, the fact remains that he completely shook Simon out of his cleats and gets open enough to score.

New England Kickoff

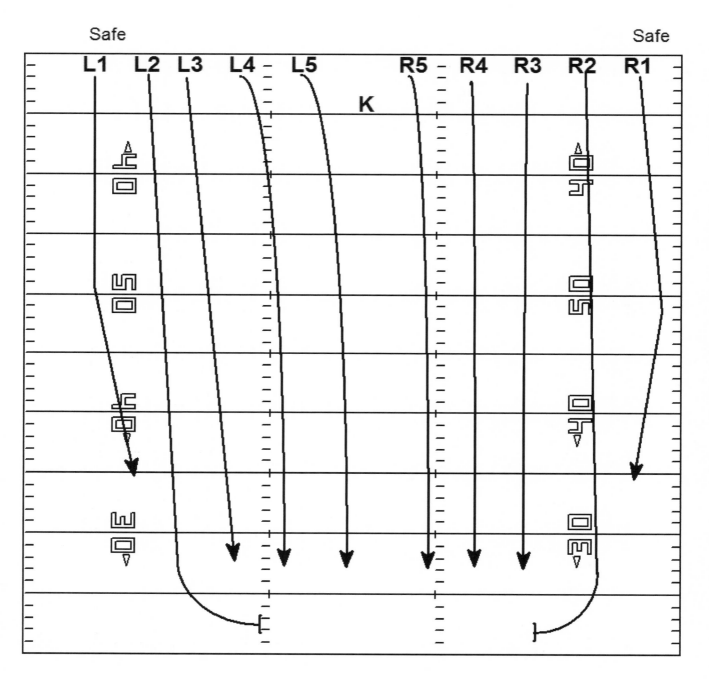

Seattle Kickoff Return

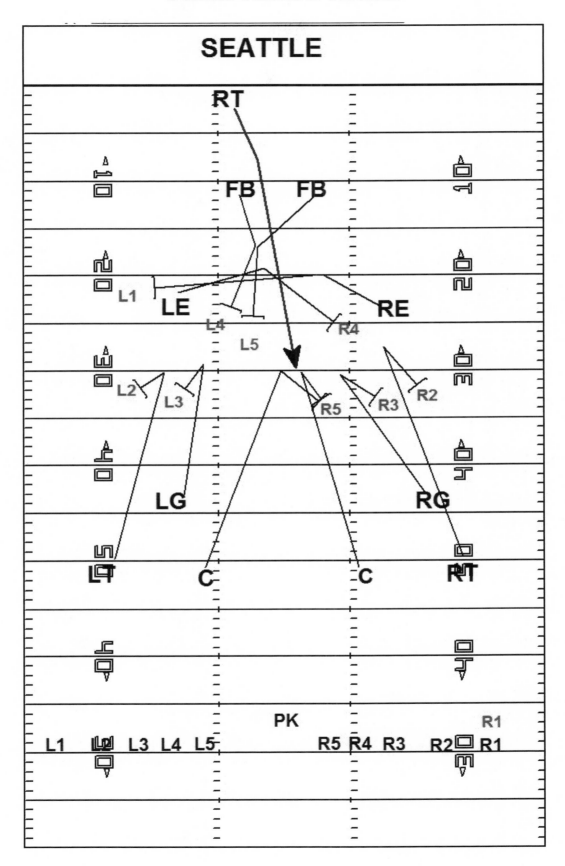

Seattle Drive 10 / Play 1 / 1ˢᵗ & 10 / -20 Yard Line / Middle / 7:55 4Q

NE – 21 SEA – 24

Summary

Pass incomplete intended for Ricardo Lockette on the deep crossing route over the middle.

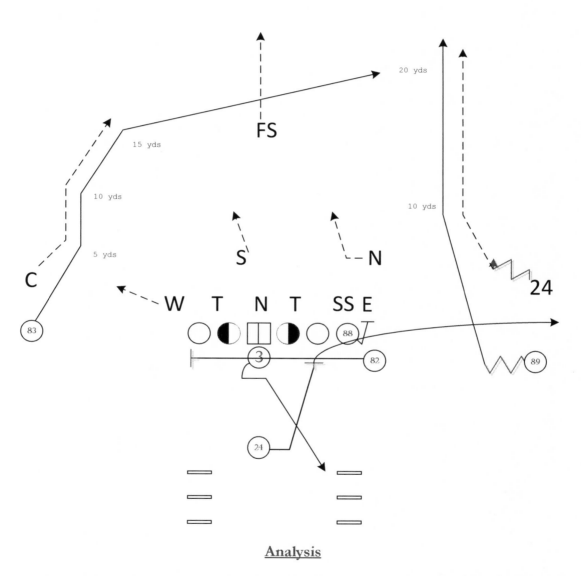

Analysis

This is one of the best throws Wilson makes all night long, but unfortunately for Seattle, Ricardo Lockette gets tripped up when trying to run away from the corner on his deep crossing route at about 20 yards down the field. With Doug Baldwin going vertical, he takes Revis and McCourty out of the equation in the middle of the field and clearing out the deep right.

The short motion brings Baldwin close enough to the two tight end wing alignment to give the defense a legitimate run threat as if he's going to crack block on an edge defender. It also gets him close to enough to the middle of the field to force McCourty to take his deep, or at the very least get in his way once Lockette catches the football on the crossing route.

The one player who plays such a big role in the play in the nickel corner Brandon Browner, who recognizes the play action pass concept, and spot drops deep down the right hash, which means that he's standing in the intended pass window, forcing Wilson to hold on to the football just a few moments longer. Seattle goes for the long ball on 1st down, nearly gets it, and ends up now in a 2nd and long situation with the tide beginning to turn in New England's favor.

Seattle Drive 10 / Play 2 / 2nd & 10 / Middle / 7:48 4Q

NE – 21 SEA – 24

Summary

Gain of 5 yards on Marshawn Lynch's carry up the middle.

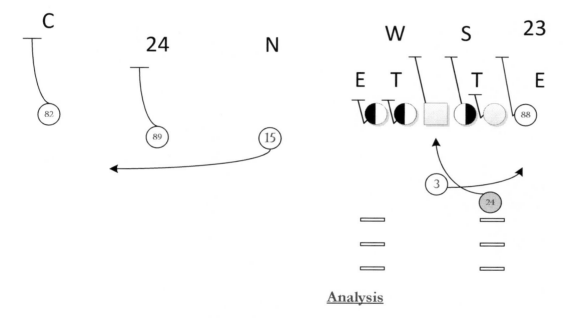

Analysis

Seattle gets back to what's worked well for them in this game, running the football out of the shotgun, especially with the attached tight end. The front that the Patriots have been giving them in this situation and against these kinds of formations, are very favorable to the run game up the middle if you can get a good jump off the snap.

The Patriots have the same cross-blitz called from last time where the Will linebacker blitzes into the opposite A-gap, and even though the Sam backer tries to get to the opposite A-gap, but since he hesitates the right guard has enough time to get a hand on him and seal him off from the play.

The defensive tackle beats the left guard at the point of attack, but not before Lynch picks up enough momentum to get 5 yards and set up 3rd and manageable.

Seattle Drive 10 / Play 3 / 3d & 5 / -25 Yard Line / Middle / 7:28 4Q

NE – 21 SEA – 24

Summary

Pass incomplete intended for Marshawn Lynch running the wheel route out of the slot.

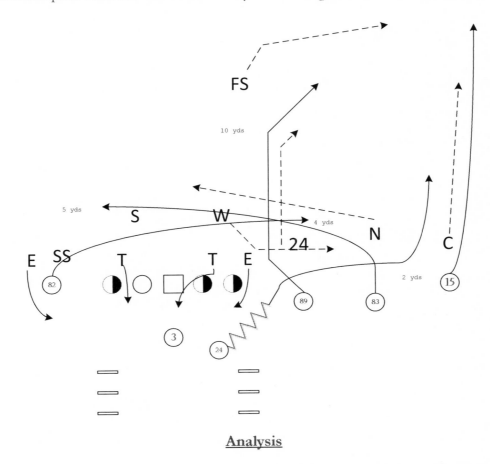

Analysis

From one end of the spectrum on 2nd down to the complete opposite direction on 3rd down. In other words, Seattle went with a very reliable play that has worked very well consistently all game long for Seattle. On this play, Darrell Bevell digs deep into his bag of tricks and comes up empty, giving the ball right back to Tom Brady. One of Marshawn Lynch's most underrated talents is his ability to catch the football, and on this play the Seahawks try to take advantage of it.

Starting off in the trips formation that has served them so well in the game, they send Marshawn Lynch in motion from the backfield to his final alignment about 2 yards off the hip of the right tackle. He's assigned to run underneath the two routes who start off breaking to the inside then he'll turn up once he gets past the numbers. The offense runs another "rub" pattern hoping to free up one of their playmakers against aggressive man coverage.

This is reminiscent of the play Seattle tried to get to Jermain Kearse down the left sideline on another 3rd down two drives earlier in the game. The technique by the #2 receiver is even the same, as he slants out aiming inside, then stopping his feel and establishing himself at a certain point, and making himself as big a target as possible to give Lynch an aiming point to run at and hopefully lose the defender.

Russell Wilson encounters a lot of pressure however, and as he's flushed to the left he's forced to let the football go off of his back foot without really putting his body behind it. Although Lynch is still blanketed by the defender he was trying to lose on the play, it probably wouldn't have mattered whether he was wide open or not, since the pass come out a little softer than expected, and behind Lynch as well.

Seattle Punt

PRO PUNT 54 STACK

3   4   5   5   4   3   2 1

1

2

New England Punt Return

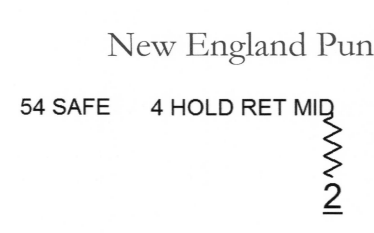

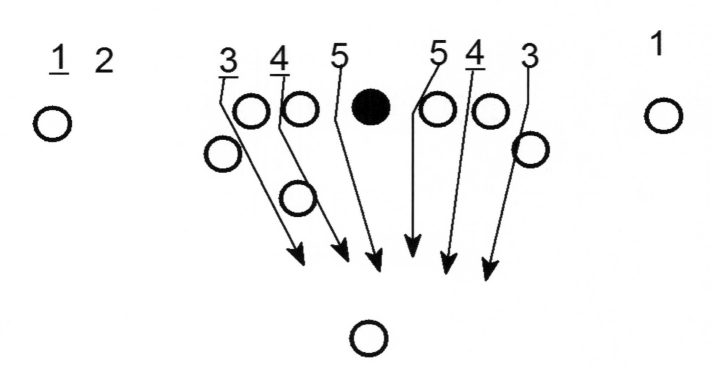

Seattle Drive #10 Review

This drive plays out similar to the last one, with the exception of 1st down, when Bevell calls a play action concept that's been circled on his call sheet for a situation like this. New England has played pretty aggressively against the run on 1st and 2nd down, so by bringing in 12 personnel and throwing the deep crossing route that's a pretty simple read for Wilson once the Z's vertical route clears out the coverage to that side of the field.

However, because the Patriots have stayed in their base nickel personnel, they have enough bodies in coverage to shrink the passing lanes. In this case, Brandon Browner #39 drops down the right hash and ends up forcing Wilson to hold onto the football a half-second longer than he wants to. As a result, the pass is off-target, and Seattle has to dig themselves out of 2nd and long with the pressure mounting.

The call on 3rd down is just as telling, with Bevel reaching deep down into the bag of tricks and calling an unfamiliar play because Belichick has done such a good job of taking away the things Seattle is most comfortable with.

New England Drive 10 / Play 1 / 1ˢᵗ & 10 / -36 Yard Line / Right Hash / 6:52 4Q

NE – 21 SEA – 24

Summary

Pass completed to Vereen underneath for a gain of 8 yards.

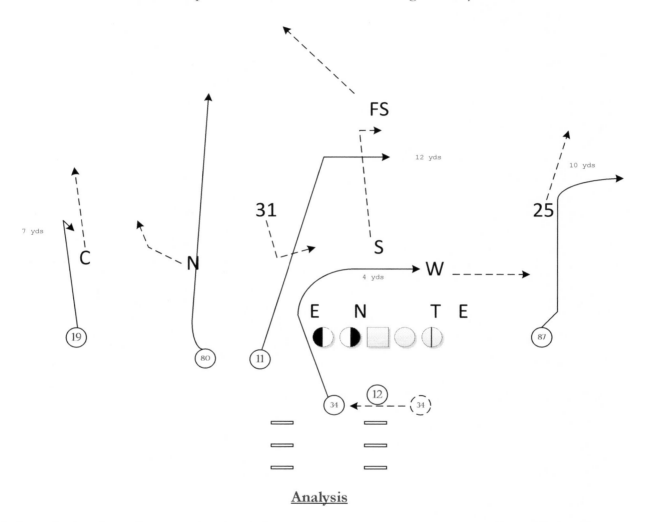

Analysis

This is an interesting adjustment by the defense to Gronkowski lined up in a slightly tighter split to the single receiver side. Because of the tight split, Seattle can use one of their linebackers to cut underneath any vertical route by Gronk, and for Sherman to play over the top with inside leverage. Brady adjusts Vereen's position and route out of the backfield by having him switch his shallow route to begin and end on opposite sides.

New England is running an adapted version of the drive concept with Edelman running the basic cross/dig route and Vereen comes out of the backfield to run the underneath route.

Brady takes the snap, and recognizing the soft coverage by Sherman, he starts eyeing Gronk's route while keeping track of the backer playing underneath of the route. This allows Vereen to get to his assigned spot, which ends up attacking where the linebacker used to be.

New England Drive 10 / Play 2 / 2ⁿᵈ & 2 / -44 Yard Line / Right Hash / 6:36 4Q

NE – 21 SEA – 24

Summary

Pass completed to Vereen in the left flat for a gain of 5 yards and a first down.

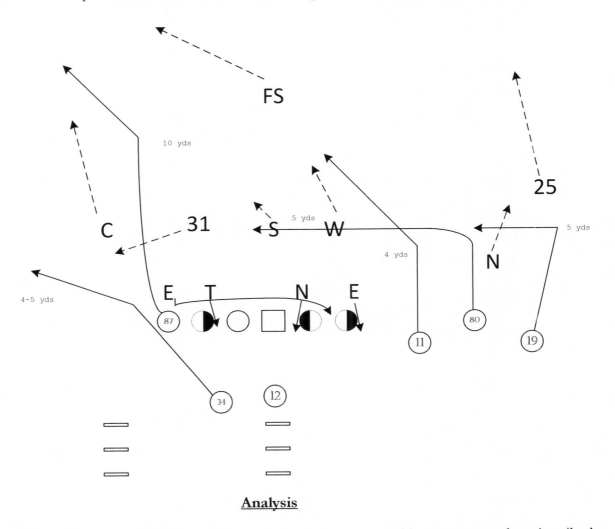

Analysis

This is a very easy read for Brady because of the way the play is set up. This concept attacks primarily the short middle (though in this case the ball ends up going to Vereen out in the left flat), but with the corner route by Gronkowski serving as a "rub" route to that side, it forces Chancellor, who is lined up inside the tackle box to have to fight to get to the flat to cover Vereen.

If either of those guys are covered, there are a pair of routes coming in from the right side to replace the man defending the flat route, and high-low the remaining inside linebacker. Finally the backside route by LaFell can provide the final outlet opportunity as he cuts across the face of the nickel defenders.

New England Drive 10 / Play 3 / 1ˢᵗ & 10 / -49 Yard Line / Left Hash / 5:52 4Q

NE – 21 SEA – 24

Summary

Pass complete to Edelman in the left flat for a gain of 9 yards.

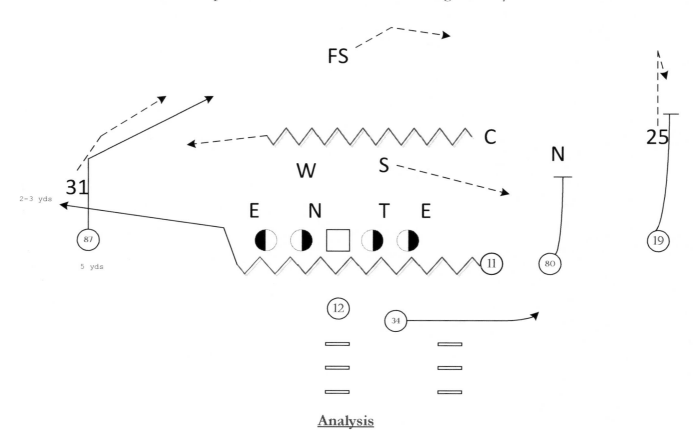

Analysis

This is similar to the play that New England ran on the first drive, where they put Edelman in motion across the formation and looking to get him open in the flat by forcing his defender to come over the top of a slant route that's more sacrificial than an actual intended target.

The reason they've split Gronk out this time is because of the kinds of coverages Seattle has played whenever he's been split out in different places during the game. This is why the process of asking questions of the defense during the first drive is important to continue throughout the game. As a coach you've got to be able to confirm your theories that you've come up with through film study during preparation and by watching the defense through the game. Based on what Seattle has shown, Josh McDaniels knows what to expect in this situation.

What he doesn't want in this situation is a coverage that will switch up responsibilities between two defensive backs on the slant route that breaks inside, and the flat player breaks out. He needs the matchup to stay the same, otherwise the whole reason New England ran the play to begin with is negated, and Brady has to flip it out to Vereen on the slow screen to the right.

New England Drive 10 / Play 4 / 2ⁿᵈ & 1 / +42 Yard Line / Left Hash / 5:39 4Q

NE – 21 SEA – 24

Summary

Pass complete to Vereen in the right flat for a gain of 6 yards, but the play is called back for offensive pass interference.

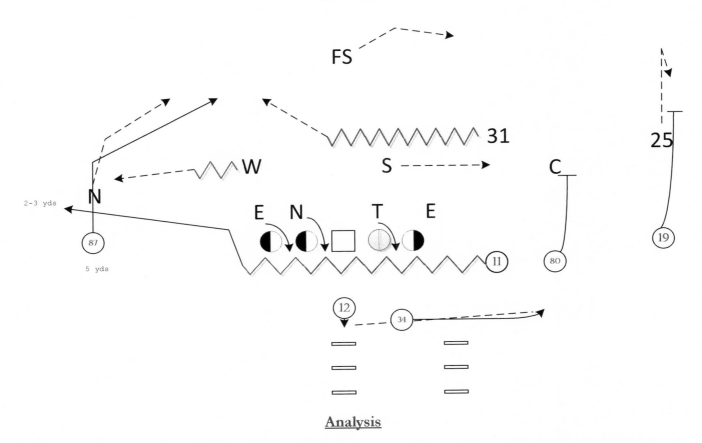

Analysis

The Patriots lines up and runs the exact same play again, only this time Gronkowski finds himself matched up on a nickel corner and a linebacker who bumped out to widen with Edelman and undercut any in-breaking route by Gronk. This of course negates a lot of the advantage of running the pass pattern to the left, since the "rub" that the Patriots are trying to create won't exist because of the coverage to that side.

Brady spots Chancellor lined up over Edelman before the snap to the 3 receiver side, and as he goes in motion, Chancellor moves into the left side of the tackle box and lets the linebacker bump out to the edge and widen out with Edelman.

As a result Brady immediately turns and fires to Vereen who is running a flare screen. He manages to pick up enough yardage for the 1st down, but the play is called back because of offensive pass interference on the blocking downfield.

New England Drive 10 / Play 5 / 2nd & 11 / -48 Yard Line / Right Hash / 4:47 4Q

NE – 21 SEA – 24

Summary

Pass complete to Gronkowski over the middle for a gain of 20 yards and a first down.

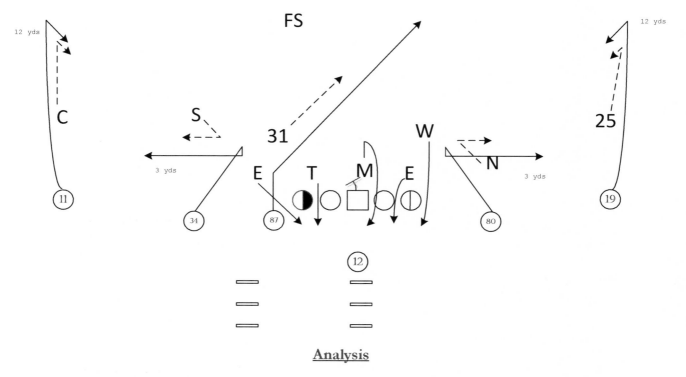

Analysis

Now the Patriots are behind schedule on the drive once again. After picking up 9 yards on 1st down, a penalty puts them in a hole on 2nd down, with 11 yards left to go.

The Mike linebacker comes on a delayed blitz, reading the center, and firing through the opposite gap once the center commits to blocking to the right.

On this play, Seattle gambles and they end up on the losing end. With the empty formation on the field, the Seahawk defense brings five men against five offensive linemen. The only problem is that now Kam Chancellor has to keep Rob Gronkowski from beating him to the inside, which he fails to do, meaning that Gronk is running uncontested down the middle, right where the inside backers used to be. Brady finds him and Gronk uses his momentum and huge frame to bowl over defenders en route to a huge gain, and more importantly, a 1st down.

New England Drive 10 / Play 6 / 1st & 10 / +32 Yard Line / Right Hash / 4:26 4Q

NE – 21 SEA – 24

Summary

Pass complete to Vereen underneath in the right flat but he's only able to get back to the original line of scrimmage.

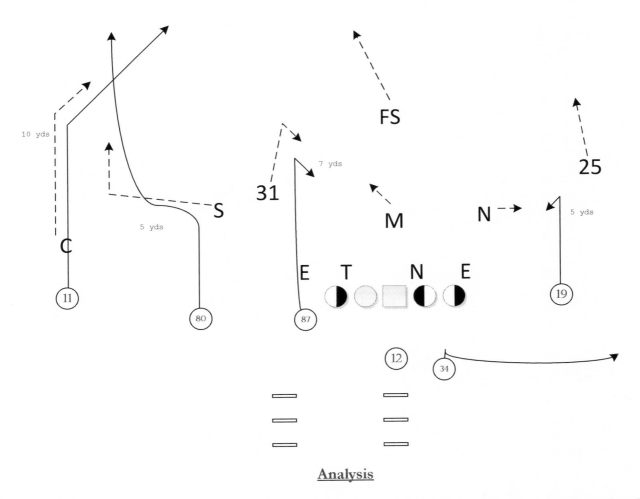

Analysis

The defense gives New England a similar look to the single receiver side to the one they played when Gronkowski lined up to that side in a tight split, where Sherman and the underneath defender to that side will bracket the receiver, with the underneath guy running out to the flat to undercut any vertical route.

This means that by taking the short hitch route by LaFell and combining it with the check-release route by Vereen, you can create a "rub" concept to free up Vereen on the edge.

Sherman's speed is one of the reasons this play is limited to no gain after starting out so promising. Brady checks the Mike linebacker's drop, and as he opens up to Gronk's side, it's an easy decision to make.

New England Drive 10 / Play 7 / 2ⁿᵈ & 10 / +32 Yard Line / Right Hash / 4:19 4Q

NE – 21 SEA – 24

Summary

Pass complete to Gronkowski for a gain of 12 yards and a first down.

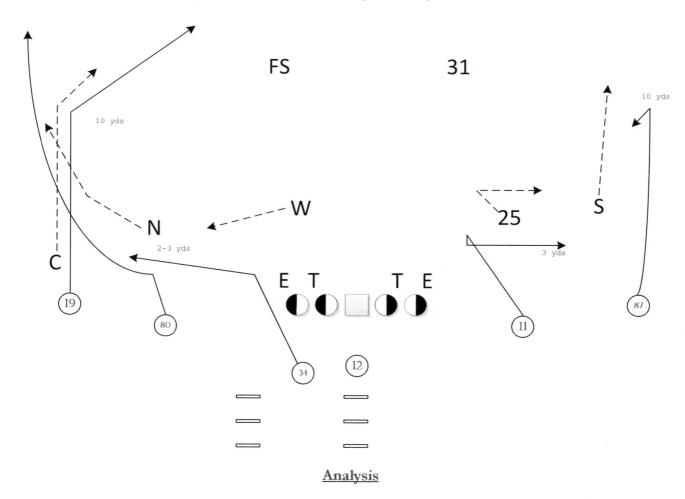

Analysis

The Patriots continue to use Gronkowski to play games with the Seattle pass coverage. With Sherman lined up over Edelman in the slot, and the linebacker playing soft coverage to the inside of Gronkowski it's unlikely there will be anyone playing underneath Gronk when he goes vertical, since this is a 2-deep man coverage look for the defense.

This time it's a simple pitch-and-catch from Brady to Gronk for the 1st down, and now New England is inside the Red Zone, well into field goal range to be able to tie the game, and possibly take the lead if they can keep up this momentum.

New England Drive 10 / Play 8 / 1ˢᵗ & 10 / +20 Yard Line / Right Hash / 3:43 4Q

NE – 21 SEA – 24

Summary

Gain of 8 yards on Vereen's run up the middle.

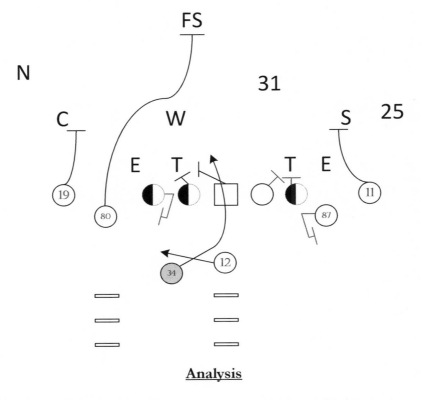

Analysis

Great job by the Patriots catching the defense off guard with the draw play here.

Traditionally, New England, as well as many other teams, have used this compressed formation to create opportunities to the outside, since by packing the defense in tight, the offense can more easily get the edge and get the football out in space to a playmaker.

This play really comes at an opportune time for New England, since Seattle lines up with both defensive tackles playing in the B gaps, with no one covering the center, meaning that there will be far less resistance up the middle in the run game until you get to the linebacker level.

Vereen is very quick, and helps set up his own blocking by getting straight downhill right away behind the center before cutting back to the left as he gets past the center, which brings the will linebacker close to the combo block.

New England Drive 10 / Play 9 / 2ⁿᵈ & 2 / +12 Yard Line / Middle / 3:15 4Q

NE – 21 SEA – 24

Summary

Pass complete to LaFell out near the left sideline for a gain of 6 yards and a first down.

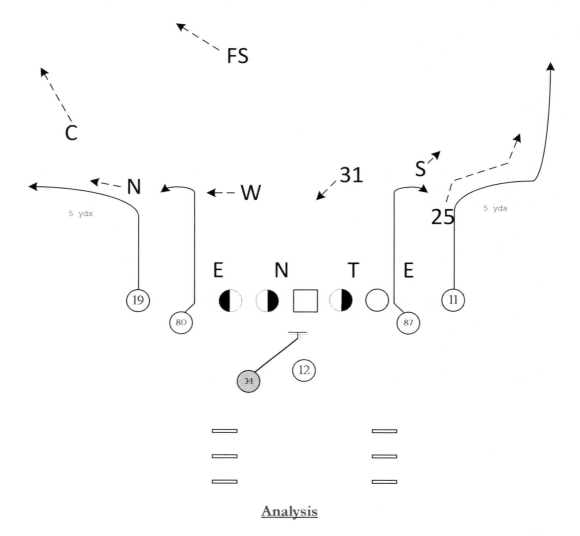

Analysis

Brady is reading the nickel to the left side and watching which route he covers. He waits just a split-second longer than originally intended since he at first widens with LaFell before crashing back down inside on Amendola. Brady's hesitation, while being the correct and conservative decision, ultimately makes the difference between LaFell catching the football 4 yards from the sideline and 2 yards from the sideline, which would've given him enough room to change direction and turn up the sideline for the score.

The play is set up so that Brady can pick a side pre-snap, but can reset and look to the opposite side if nothing's open. Since the Patriots aren't stupid, they're obviously not going to risk testing Sherman on a simple out pattern, so instead they'll try a double move to that side.

The reason for calling this play was to look for a high-percentage throw to pick up the 1st down on 2nd and 2, so Brady's 1st look is going to be throwing the simple routes on the simple read.

If the simple routes aren't open to the left side, the double move to the right by Edelman is designed to open up space underneath for the route by Gronk and maybe even create some separation for Edelman from Sherman.

New England Drive 10 / Play 10 / 1ˢᵗ & Goal / +6 Yard Line / Left Hash / 2:52 4Q

NE – 21 SEA – 24

Summary

Gain of 3 yards on Blount's run up the middle.

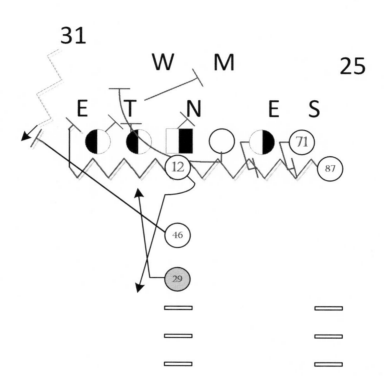

Analysis

Gronkowski does a great job of sticking his inside foot in the ground winning the inside gap to open up a hole for the right guard pulling around, who has just enough room to fit off-tackle, but he's tripped up as he comes through the gap.

Meanwhile Blount stays straight downhill on his north-south angle before cutting to the left off of the combo in the 3 technique tackle, and puts his head down to pick up what he can. Even though Seattle flies to the football, Blount manages to cut the distance between the offense and the goal line.

New England Drive 10 / Play 11 / 2nd & Goal / +3 Yard Line / Left Hash / 2:23 4Q

NE – 21 SEA – 24

Summary

Touchdown! Pass complete to Julian Edelman in the left flat for a gain of 3 yards and a score.

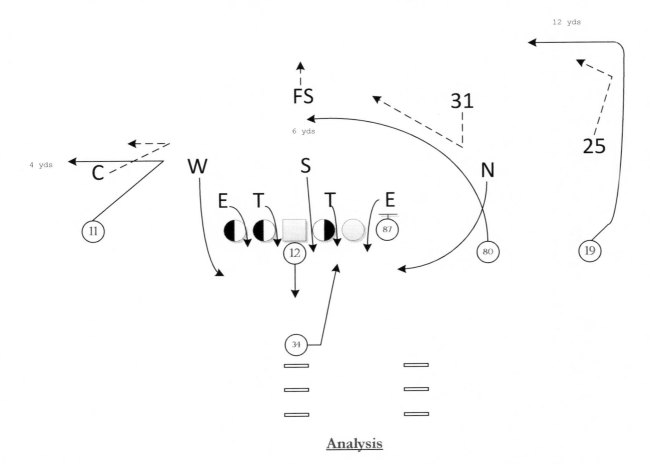

Analysis

Now that the Patriots are back inside the five yard line, they can go right back to the play that they should've scored on during the previous trip down in this area.

The depth of the route by Edelman means that in order to be able to run and fades into the end zone he has to start off from the five yard line or closer than that so that he can naturally fade into the end zone off of the cut back inside.

The other marked difference on this play is that Brady completely abandons the play fake and stares down Edelman's route waiting to break to the outside.

Seattle comes with the cover 0 blitz on this play, with Earl Thomas sitting over the top of Gronkowski, who stays in to block. The Seahawks bring pressure with 6 guys in to block, which gives Brady enough time to get Edelman the football for a score that gives the Patriots the lead once again.

New England PAT/ Seattle PAT Block

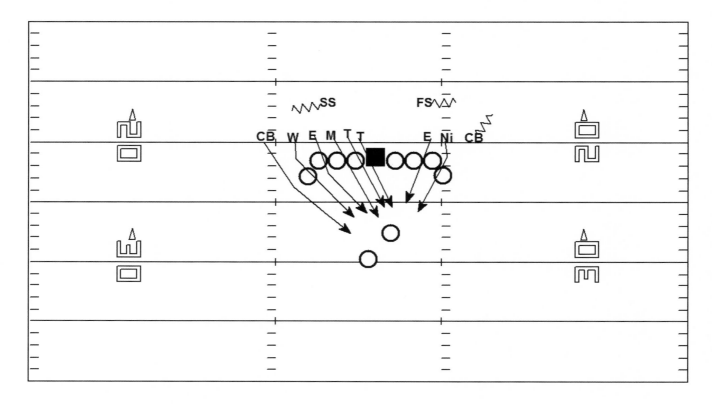

New England Drive #10 Review

Like most of the successful drives for New England in this game, Shane Vereen was a big part of the Patriots' journey to the end zone.

As Brady continues to target Vereen underneath early in the drive, the defense starts to creep up and play tighter, which opens up space behind the coverage for Gronkowski at midfield.

The drive has elements of successful part of the New England game plan, including attacking the single receiver side of the formation, using compressed formation to create space on the outside of the formation.

The final play of the drive goes right back to a throw Brady messed in this spot on the last drive, but Brady doesn't miss twice.

Edelman is wide open for the score and New England takes the late lead.

New England Kickoff

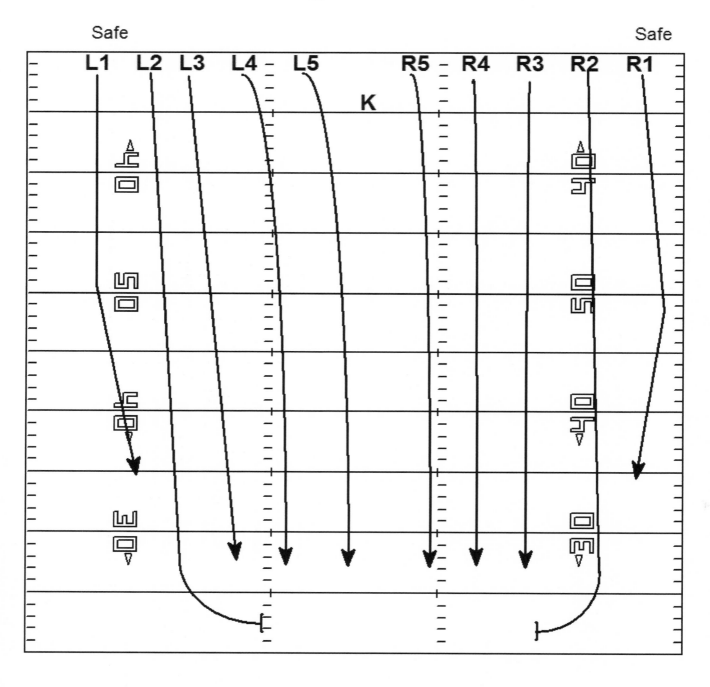

Seattle Kickoff Return

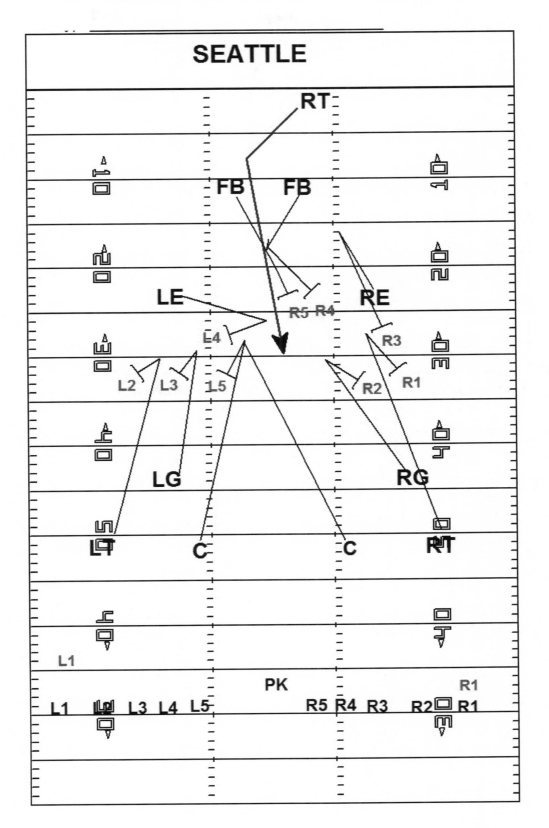

Seattle Drive 11 / Play 1 / 1ˢᵗ & 10 / -20 Yard Line / Middle / 2:02 4Q

NE – 28 SEA – 24

Summary

Pass complete deep down the left sideline to Marshawn Lynch for a 31 yard gain and a first down.

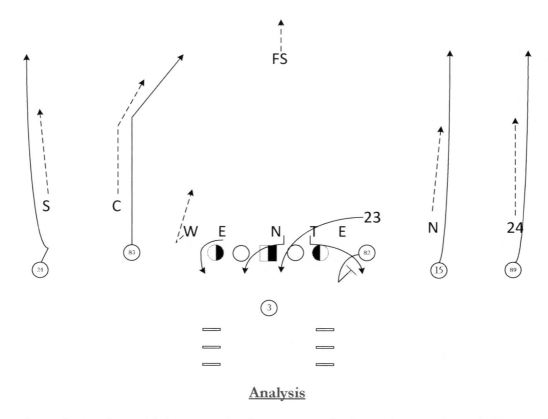

Analysis

Seattle, now down four points with just over 2 minutes to go, looks to the guy they tried to get the football to the last time this offense was on the field. The offensive personnel stays the same it's been for much of the game, 11 personnel group, only this time they do what New England has made a habit of doing in this game, moving the running back Lynch out wide to the left and seeing how the defense reacts.

In this case, the Patriots send Jamie Collins with him out wide in man-to-man coverage.

The corner playing in the slot over the top of #83 Lockette just inside of Lynch in the formation starts dropping before the snap and has his back turned completely to the sideline. The implications are clear, there really is no help coming for Collins when defending Lynch, however as the slot corner is backpedaling into position and working on a deeper drop, he is still technically in position to help on the vertical route developing outside of him if he sees the ball in the air as he's dropping back to his spot. Therefore, to truly free up Lynch the offseason has to remove the slot corner from the equation by having the receiver start to break inside on a skinny post, and based on the way he's running the route, he looks like he's preparing to cut inside on the dig.

Seattle is trying to set up their offense to look like the drive concept is coming from the 2 receiver side, and they do a great job of it. As Lynch stutter-steps inside for a moment to give the look of a shallow crossing route, he shakes Collins just enough as he gets vertical, giving Russell Wilson the window he needs to hit Lynch with the long ball.

All of a sudden Seattle is in New England territory with 2 minutes to go.

Seattle Drive 11 / Play 2 / 1ˢᵗ & 10 / +49 Yard Line / Left Hash / 1:55 4Q

NE – 28 SEA – 24

Summary

Pass incomplete intended for Jermaine Kearse running a seam route down the middle of the field.

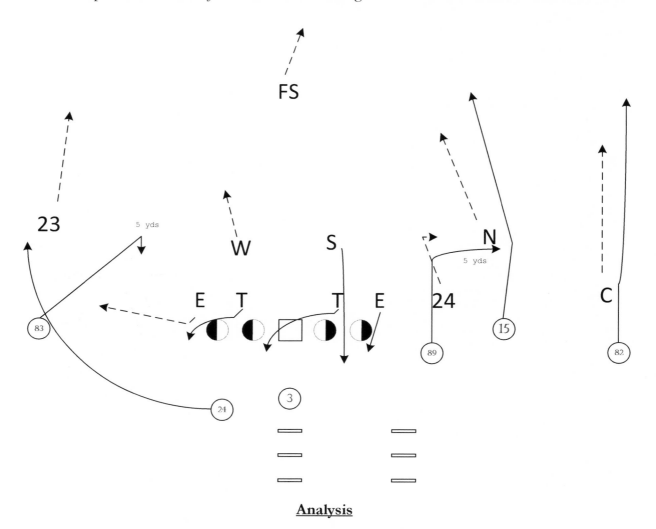

Analysis

Chandler Jones drops with Lynch to the right side as he's running with the flare route. New England wants to win the numbers game to both sides in the passing game, and this is a great way to do it.

However, on this play Russell Wilson is looking for the long ball again, since McCourty is leaning to the left and New England has two receivers going vertical to the right side of the formation.

Wilson attempts to fire the ball in there at the intermediate level of the pass game, once Jermaine Kearse makes a move on the nickel corner across from him, Malcolm Butler. Wilson is a little late on the throw, as he waited too long after Kearse made his move to the inside which gave Butler time to recover and knock down the pass from behind.

Seattle Drive 11 / Play 3 / 2nd & 10 / +49 Yard Line / Middle / 1:50 4Q

NE – 28 SEA – 21

Summary

Pass incomplete intended for Chris Matthews in the deep right side of the field.

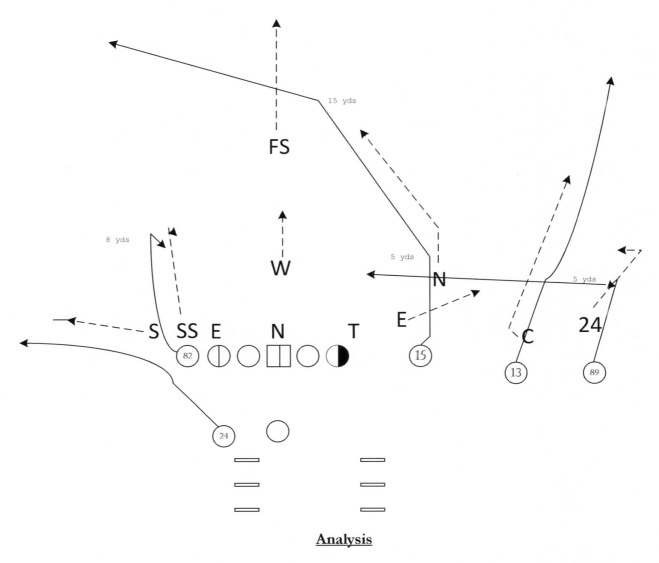

Analysis

Once again Seattle calls this pass play from earlier in the game. Wilson's 1st read is to the deep crossing route side, since with the leverage Kearse has on the defender, there's at least a 50/50 chance for a big play. On the other hand, Kearse had a step on Butler on the previous play, and Butler was able to use his recovery speed to knock the pass away at the last moment, not to mention that McCourty is playing over the top of the crossing route to the left side.

Conversely, the receivers to the right side of the field are both playing one-on-one, with the free safety over to the other side of the field. Chris Matthews is running a fade route deep to the right side after originally lining up in the slot to create more space to the outside as he gets deeper in the route.

Wilson takes a shot deep down the right side of the field, but doesn't put enough on it, meaning that Matthews has to try to come back for the ball, meaning that Brandon Browner can close the gap between he and Matthews, and knock the pass away.

Seattle Drive 11 / Play 4 / 3rd & 10 / +49 Yard Line / Middle / 1:41 4Q

NE – 28 SEA – 24

Summary

Pass complete to Ricardo Lockette for a gain of 11 yards and a 1st down.

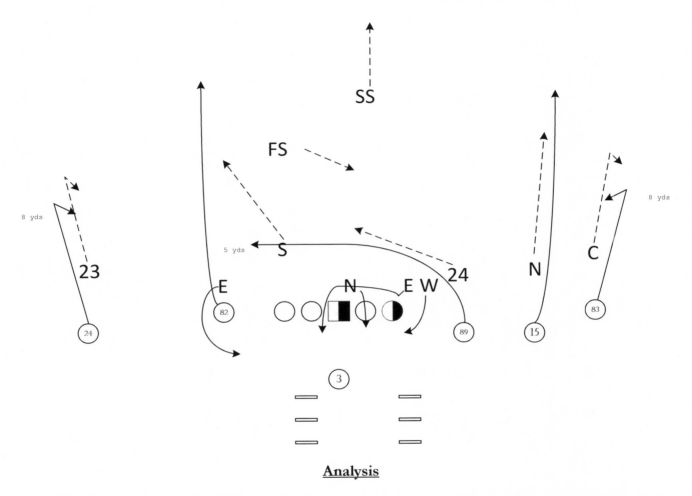

Analysis

A slightly different twist on a concept Seattle has been running all game long, the expanding hitch toward the sideline, with seam routes out of the slot to either side to free up the hitch routes to the outside as much as possible. The is in addition to Doug Baldwin being placed in the slot and running a drag route across the middle of the field in order to take Revis completely out of the play, away from where they really wanted to go with the football, which was to the outside.

Once again Wilson gets the pass off a little late, but he still gets it to Lockette on the hitch route to the right, who manages to evade the corner Logan Ryan long enough to pick up the extra couple of yards after the catch for the first down.

New England is in the nickel defense, and moves to a robber coverage as the offense comes out in empty, assuming that Seattle is going to try to attack the middle of the field on 3rd and long, using simple throws and routes, maybe to set up 4th down, since they're obviously not going to punt.

However Darrell Bevell and Russell Wilson are looking to the same concept they've relied on many times during the game, and it works out for them once again.

Seattle Drive 11 / Play 5 / 1st & 10 / +38 Yard Line / Right Hash / 1:25 4Q

NE – 28 SEA – 24

Summary

Pass complete to Jermaine Kearse down the right sideline for of a gain of 33 yards and a first down.

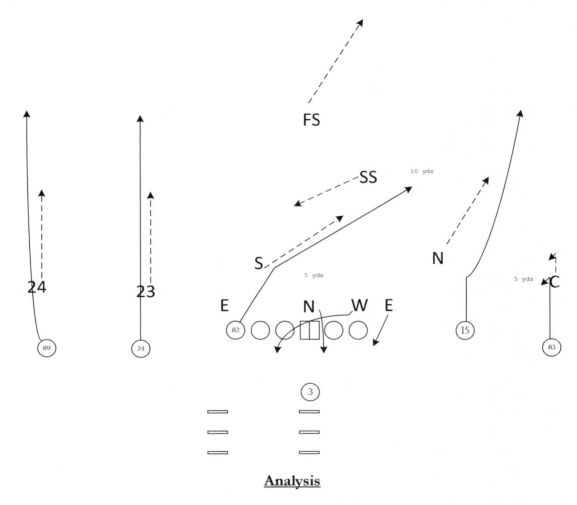

Analysis

Now that Seattle has their 1st down, they have a little bit more breathing room and Bevell decides to take another shot down the field, in what turns out to be a tremendous individual play by Jermaine Kearse.

Having gleaned what he can from earlier parts of this drive, Bevell knows two things: 1) The New England defense is going to try to crowd the middle of the field against an empty formation to take away any short crossing routes or any other kinds of easy throws, and 2) the fade route by Chris Matthews from the slot should've been caught, since it was simple one-on-one coverage. Knowing that, the Seahawks line up in empty again, with a play designed to attack the deep right side.

The tight end Luke Wilson comes across on a medium-depth crossing route to occupy the defense in the middle of the field and hopefully influences the safety. Meanwhile, Jermain Kearse runs his vertical release, then starts to 'fade' away to the sideline once he's past the depth of the hitch route by Lockette. It should be noted that the free safety is playing a lot more centered than on previous plays, since with Marshawn Lynch lined up in the left slot, as well as Revis playing to that side, the defense isn't quite as worried about giving help to that side.

Malcolm Butler initially gets a hand on the pass, seemingly knocking it away, but thanks to a fortuitous bounce off of Butler's fingertips the ball lands squarely in Kearse's chest as he falls to the ground, and he manages to corral it for the big play. At this moment, it seems like the Patriots are in danger of losing another Super Bowl late thanks to a miraculous pass and catch.

Seattle Drive 11 / Play 6 / 1st & Goal / +5 Yard Line / Right Hash / 1:06 4Q

NE – 28 SEA – 24

Summary

Gain of 4 yards on the carry by Lynch along the left side.

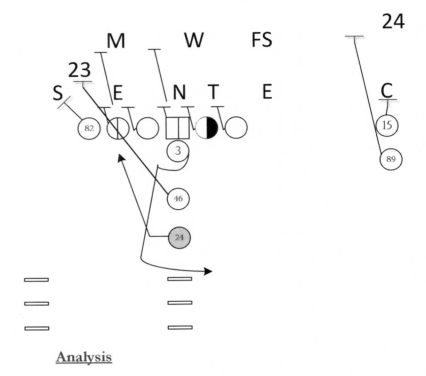

Analysis

When you have Marshawn Lynch inside the five yard line, down four points, it's a great weapon to have available.

The clock has stopped, meaning that Seattle doesn't have to use a timeout to make personnel adjustments, so they take a receiver off the field and bring on the fullback #46 Will Tukuafu as an extra body to use at the point of attack in the run game.

Seattle has had some good success out of the I-Formation, especially running to the left, and away from Vince Wilfork on the right side. This time is no different.

The left tackle #76 Russell Okung and left guard #77 James Carpenter works in conjunction with one another to create a seal to the inside of the C gap, meanwhile the tight end Luke Wilson and the fullback Tukuafu seals off the outside of the C-gap, creating a big running lane for Lynch between the tackle and tight end spot.

The only thing that keeps this from being a score is that Dante Hightower, the Mike stacked over the left tackle, manages to shed Okung's block and get to Lynch to bring him down at the one yard line.

Seattle Drive 11 / Play 7 / 2ⁿᵈ & Goal / +1 Yard Line / Left Hash / 0:30 4Q

NE – 28 SEA – 24

Summary

Interception! Pass intended for Ricardo Lockette is intercepted by Malcolm Butler at the 1 yard line.

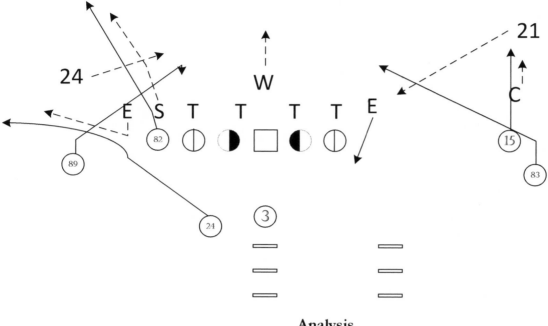

Analysis

After nearly punching the ball in on the 1 yard line, Seattle stats to think about when they should score, since they don't want to leave too much time for New England to come back and tie/win the game. At first, Seattle thinks that there's a good chance Belichick will take a timeout after Lunch is tackled at the one yard line, but he decides to let it play out.

Nevertheless, they do bring in their goal line personnel on defense, and as a result, while Pete Carroll and Darrell Bevell are letting the clock tick down to under 30 seconds, they make personnel adjustments, taking the fullback off the field and bringing on a 3rd receiver, hoping to take advantage of personnel matchups when New England has their run defenders on the field.

Wilson moves Baldwin and Lynch to the left side of the formation in order to set up the "spot" concept to the left, and also to free up space for the route on the right side he really wants to throw to Lockette.

There are no safeties on the field, unless you count the linebacker aligned over the center who is reading the backfield for his run/pass read. As he looks over the defense before the snap, Wilson knows that if Jermaine Kearse can get a good release off the line, it should create a pretty big window underneath for the slant by Lockette.

On defense, #21 Malcolm Butler knows the same thing, and he also knows he's about to get beat inside if Lockette gets inside of him and the other corner. At the snap, Lockette gives a quick stutter step to the outside with the hope of making Butler hesitate, but Butler doesn't budge. Kearse goes vertical off the line of scrimmage to try and create that seal on Butler and keep him out of the passing lane and allow Lockette to run the wide open slant underneath him.

As Wilson throws the football, everything looks for an instant like it's going according to plan, since Lockette appears to be heading for an easy score. At the last minute, Butler comes in front of the pass and intercepts it at the one yard line, making one of the all-time great plays in Super Bowl history. The Patriots are World Champions once again.

Seattle Drive #11 Review

The Seahawks aren't interested in nickel-and-diming their way down the field on the final drive, instead they continue to take shots down the field, swinging for the home run every play and hoping to hit a couple of them. The sooner they get down close to the goal line, the sooner they can open up the whole playbook and use Lynch in the run game.

Once Jermaine Kearse makes the catch inside the ten yard line, then the discussion starts to happen about how much time they should leave on the clock for New England once they score.

The run out of twins by Lynch down to the one was an attempt to score (obviously) but it was also to get the clock moving again, since Seattle had called a timeout after Kearse's big catch that got them down there.

Now as the clock starts to tick down close to 30 seconds, New England lines up with goal line personnel (6 defensive linemen, 2 linebackers, 3 defensive backs), which Pete Carroll said after the game played a big part in their decision to throw the football. According to him, the thinking was that they wanted to throw a pass into the end zone. If it was a score, then great. If it was incomplete, they would still have a timeout with 20 seconds left and a yard to go, so they could still call whatever play they wanted and the whole playbook would be open at that point.

The idea to pass was an interesting one, but it wasn't the colossal screw up that many people (including myself at the time) made it out to be. My only complaint would be with the actual play called. I would've much rather seen Wilson roll out to one side or another where he could easily run for the score or throw the ball out of the back of the end zone if need be.

Of course, all this talk about the play call ignores the fact that Malcolm Butler, even without the huge stakes involved, made an incredible play on the football, especially since he came from behind a stacked formation that was specifically designed for sealing him off from the pass being thrown.

ABOUT THE AUTHOR

As a writer who spent a period of time coaching high school and college football, Alex Kirby loves talking the X's and O's of the game, and prides himself on his ability to simplify the important details of the action without dumbing down his analysis.

He is the owner and writer at ProFootballStrategy.com and currently lives and works in Indianapolis, Indiana

ALSO WRITTEN BY ALEX KIRBY

Speed Kills: Breaking Down the Chip Kelly Offense

Inside the Auburn Offense

Every Play Revealed: Oregon vs Ohio State